D0914260

RED, WHITE AND TRUE BLUE

RED, WHITE AND TRUE BLUE
The Loyalists in the Revolution

Edited by
ESMOND WRIGHT

Published for the Institute of United States Studies

AMS PRESS
New York

FIRST AMS PRESS EDITION: 1976

Library of Congress Cataloguing in Publication Data
Main entry under title:

Red, white & true blue.

"The papers . . . were first read . . . in
November 1975."
Includes bibliographies.
1. American loyalists—Congress. I. Wright
Esmond. II. London. University. Institute of
United States Studies.
E277.R3   973.3'14   76-23976
ISBN 0-404-15400-X

CONTENTS

INTRODUCTION

The papers printed here were first read at a conference on the American Loyalists held at the Institute of United States Studies, University of London, in November 1975. It was the first Loyalist Conference held in London, matching those held in New York in 1968 in Lehigh, Pennsylvania in 1969, and in Fredericton, New Brunswick in 1972; and it was made possible by the generous support of the Leverhulme Trust, who have also for four years financed the compiling of a list of Loyalist names drawn from the archives of the Public Record Office. This British activity reflects the interest similarly shown in the Loyalists by a team of American historians, headed by Professor R. A. East of City University of New York, and Dr James Mooney of the Historical Society of Pennsylvania, and by a team of Canadian historians led by Professors Stewart McNutt and Wallace Brown of the University of New Brunswick at Fredericton. These groups form part of the Loyalist Paper Project, a plan for the assembling and publication of an interactional finding list of loyalist names that arose from a conference at CUNY in 1969, and which has had the support of the National Endowment for the Humanities in the U.S. and of the Canada Council in Canada. It represents a piece of enterprising international scholarship, tilling a little-worked field.

It is a curious comment on the American Bicentennial that what is likely to be one of its most striking by-products is this reawakened interest in those who lost by the Revolution. Yet perhaps this interest in the losers is itself a characteristic of our own tortured and uneasy times, when history is being seen by the New Left as the story told "from the bottom up," when Departments of Black Studies have been set up in many Universities, and when the story of Vietnam, the first war in which the U.S. was defeated and by a militarily inferior power, reminds many observers both of 1776 and of 1865, posing again those questions of loyalty, treason and ideology that mark all civil wars.

Until recently there has been a striking contrast between 1776 and 1861. If each was in fact a civil war, Robert E. Lee was seen as heroic even in the North—more heroic than Ulysses Grant—whereas Thomas Hutchinson, Benedict Arnold, Patrick Ferguson, Butler the Ranger and Joseph Brant have all been seen until now as double-dyed villains. Part of the mythologizing of the American Revolution demanded, it seems, the blackening (or, much more effectively, the silencing) of the Loyalists. They hardly appear in the popular and received versions, though they often appear in noble guise in the pages of novelists like Kenneth Roberts. Yet some 80,000 Loyalists emigrated in or by 1783—more, per head of the population, than exiled themselves from France in and after 1789; about 20,000 Americans fought for George III; and perhaps, in their hearts, one in five of the American people were loyal, if not fully and actively Loyalist. Some 5,000 of them filed claims as "the American Sufferers" for their losses and were rewarded with cash grants of some £3 million, plus land in Canada (of which they are the Founding Fathers), jobs in Government employment at home and abroad—if they could be found for them—or parishes if they were clergy. The British Government was generous to them. For they were one of the first of the legions of the displaced and the dispossessed who also constitute a recurring theme in modern history. The War of American Independence, with its employment of foreign mercenaries, its guerrilla battles, its experiments with rifles and with "combined ops," its harrying of civilians, its seizure of rebel estates and its columns of refugees is unhappily the first of modern wars.

As a corrective, therefore, to the spirit of jubilee that properly marks 1776, and as a piece of genuinely international and genuinely original research in the records, the Loyalist Papers merit attention. The papers printed here reflect the scale of that interest, and, I believe, the quality of the work being done.

Esmond Wright

MARCHING TO A DIFFERENT DRUMMER—
THE POLITICAL PHILOSOPHY
OF THE AMERICAN LOYALISTS

BY

ANN GORMAN CONDON

One of the curious aspects of our present understanding of the Loyalists is the absence of a clearcut, positive definition of Loyalist political philosophy. We have in recent years been provided with a series of careful, highly sympathetic studies of the Loyalists. Yet none of these has been able to detect among the Loyalist adherents either a widely-held set of political and social beliefs or a common, comprehensive vision of the future of the North American continent. As a result, Loyalist historians have had to rely on personality types and on extensive comparisons with the leaders of the revolutionary movement in order to describe their subjects. Thus Leonard W. Labaree, whose essay essentially began our modern consideration of the Loyalists, found it easiest to define the Tory or Loyalist mentality by contrasting it with its revolutionary counterpart. Participation in a revolution required, according to Labaree, "a special kind of imagination . . . a general bravery . . . a faith in the future, a power to imagine vividly . . . an optimistic disregard of possibilities of loss or of failure." Labaree felt that the Loyalists, being "pessimists" at heart, lacked this sort of courage. They were men who "saw the dangers ahead rather than the noble possibilities."¹ More than a decade later, William H. Nelson came to essentially the same conclusion: that the

1

Tories' political position was ultimately based on a fear of change, on an inability to believe either in their fellow men or in the future. Nelson wrote of the Tories that "lacking confidence both in individual men and in individual generations of men, they were suspicious of anything that broke through the crust of custom and took people out of their usual habits."[2] Subsequent studies have accepted this essentially negative description of the Loyalist approach to the world. Indeed, the most recent work in the field, Bernard Bailyn's analysis of the thought of Thomas Hutchinson, attributes the Loyalist failure to an inability to understand "the moral passion and the optimistic and idealistic impulses that gripped the minds of the Revolutionaries."[3] In short, our contemporary historians seem agreed that the Loyalists' failure to appreciate the significance of the revolutionary movement, to anticipate, as it were, the wave of the future was due to some personal deficiency on their part—some failure of perception, or imagination, or nerve—rather than to the fact that the Loyalists were committed to a different mode of development for the North American continent.

Yet surely this is curious. How is it that the Loyalist political leaders—men who were not only among the most sophisticated, knowledgeable and involved members of their own colonies, but who were often conversant as well with the intricate political and commercial operations of the British empire—how is it that these urbane, savvy individuals should prove so utterly barren when it came to positive political beliefs or aspirations for the future? I would like to argue in this paper that they were not, and that our inability to identify a positive Loyalist political philosophy arises because we have not yet discovered a suitable frame of reference for comprehending the Loyalist experience. As part of my search for this elusive frame of reference, I wish particularly to explore two concepts central to both the Loyalists and to Loyalist historiography: empire and liberty.

Neglect of the Loyalists by historians in the first half of the nineteenth century was followed by attempts to relate Loyalist attitudes on empire to the emerging concept of imperialism. Such efforts have in the long run obscured Loyalist political thought and rendered its identification more difficult. For the term imperialism entered the twentieth century with a bad image, and has become increasingly unpopular ever since. From the concentration camps of the Boer War to the plantations of Latin America to the "fire zones" of Vietnam, imperialism has time and again proven itself to be such an instrument of greed and wanton disregard for human dignity that it has earned the condemnation of Marxist and non-Marxist critics alike. Indeed the epithets hurled at imperialists by those whom they oppresses— gringos, running dogs, pigs—have been seen to contain such a large element of truth that imperialism ranks today only slightly below totalitarianism or the Final Solution in our western catechism of political sins. Given this prevailing cultural attitude, it is difficult for the modern observer to admire a group of men like the Loyalists who made the defense and preservation of the British empire their most important political principle.

The first Loyalist historians were themselves imperialists of the most jingoistic, racially pretentious sort, and they tended to invest their Loyalist subjects with their own cultural prejudices. In Canada, as Carl Berger has shown, these original Loyalist historians formed the core of the Imperial Federation League and, with filiopietistic devotion, they glorified their Loyalist ancestors in order to prove that the new Canadian Confederation possessed a heroic past and that they, the direct descendants of the Loyalist founders, were ordained by history to govern Canadian society.[4] Professor Bailyn has noticed a similar phenomenon in the United States, where such Loyalist historians as Sidney G. Fisher and James K. Hosmer identified themselves with both the Loyalists and with British political institutions in reaction against the changing racial character of America and the rising dominance of the political boss and the finance capitalist.[5] In both countries, these early historians tended to distort their picture of the Loyalists by placing exaggerated emphasis on their aristocratic and martial virtues—their family background and education, their manners, their bravery, their sense of honor and devotion to principle. To an important extent, the Kiplingesque image which these nineteenth-century historians gave to the Loyalists—as some sort of Anglo-Saxon conquistadors—still persists today.

For this reason, it is necessary to stress that, whatever problems their descendants may have had, the Loyalists themselves did not by any stretch of the imagination resemble such advocates of aggressive imperialism as Cecil Rhodes or Theodore Roosevelt. Although the Loyalists certainly wanted to develop the British imperial possessions in North America, their imperial philosophy most emphatically did not include—did not even ever consider—forced labor or any of the other techniques of control and exploitation which later generations would develop in contempt of the people under their jurisdiction.

The Loyalists' view of the empire was entirely different from these later manifestations of imperialism, and until this difference is explicitly recognized, our ability to appreciate their historical contribution will be necessarily limited. To put this difference as starkly as possible, the Loyalists envisaged an empire whose unifying bond would be the British system of constitutional government, while the imperialists of the late nineteenth century and after carved out their empires by the application of superior force. The one was characterized by a mutuality of interests and respect, the other's most prominent features were mastery and exploitation.

The Loyalists dreamed of an Anglo-American empire in which the mother country and the colonies would work together to develop and exchange the economic, political and cultural advantages they shared. Great Britain would supply her superior commercial channels, her well developed constitutional system, and her naval supremacy. The colonists would offer the abundant natural resources of their rich continent, the energy of their young and growing population, and the markets which both these resources and this population would generate. Each would live under the same constitutional form of government; each would respect the political rights of the other; each would integrate its economy into this imperial system so that both would enjoy its benefits; each would contribute to the common defense, and the King's ultimate sovereignty would provide the reinforcing link to the entire system.

This dream of an Anglo-American empire did not begin with the Loyalists; in fact it antedated the American Revolution by at least twenty years. During the decade of the 1750s, the actual economic potential of the North American continent and the growing political maturity of the British American colonies became increasingly apparent to farsighted men on both sides of the Atlantic. It also became apparent that the old, loose ties between Britain and her individual colonies would no longer suffice and that a new, more integrated imperial structure was needed. Benjamin Franklin's Albany Plan of 1754 was the first attempt to organize the colonies into a single political unit which would deal on a collective basis with the imperial authorities. In succeeding years, many other men from both Great Britain and the colonies wrestled with the problem of developing new political forms that would recognize the colonies' increased maturity and give them a more substantive voice in setting imperial policy. William Shirley, William Pitt the elder, the young Lord Shelburne, and Thomas Pownall were among those who saw the promise of an Anglo-American empire and tried to fashion policies that might bring this promise to fruition. On the American side, Franklin was the earliest, most persistent advocate of a new imperial order, and when he became disenchanted, the cause was taken up by men like William Smith, jr., and Joseph Galloway.

These proponents of a new, more equal, mutually beneficial Anglo-American union were the intellectual progenitors of the Loyalist movement. They were characterized on the one hand by a fervent belief in the potential greatness of America and, on the other, by an acute awareness of the newness, the crudeness of North American society. As active participants in colonial affairs, these eventual Loyalists knew firsthand the centrifugal impulses which threatened community life on their continent— the immaturity of its institutions, the shortage of trained leadership, the high value placed by the frontier on sheer physical strength, the threat to social cohesion posed by the abundance of free land, the fragile economic and military security. And they believed that the promise of America could only be realized if a sufficiently strong bulwark were present on the continent to resist these centrifugal impulses and impose stability. This bulwark was, of course, Great Britain, with her well developed system of constitutional government, her economic and military strength, and her rich cultural resources. Although Loyalist political leaders often criticized specific British policies towards the colonies, they worked nevertheless to retain and enlarge the British connection in America because they were convinced that the power and the traditions of the empire could offer the inhabitants of their rough, sprawling continent a quality of life that was safer, richer, more stable—and even freer—than any they could hope to provide for themselves in the foreseeable future.

I stress the word freer: the Loyalists as a group were certainly as concerned with the preservation of American liberty as any member of colonial society. They disagreed with their revolutionary counterparts, however, on the question of where the real danger to colonial liberty lay. Those who supported American independence tended to regard government—public authority—as the principal threat to personal liberty. Thus, the galvanizing force behind the revolutionary movement was the conviction that the British ministry of the day was engaged in a calculated campaign to reduce colonial liberty. Thus also, the Bill of Rights which the victorious revolutionaries appended to their Constitution in 1789 was primarily concerned with defining those inviolable areas of human conduct which government may not touch without becoming tyrannical. By contrast, the Loyalist frame of mind perceived that liberty could be threatened from below as well as from above, that a mob, for example, could take away property as well as a ministry, that a committee could violate conscience as well as a king, that men could be deprived of their personal peace and security by the absence of authority as well as its abuse. And in the Loyalists' judgment, the greatest danger to liberty on the North American continent came in fact from below. Whatever its occasional excesses, the British government, separated as it was by 3000 miles of ocean and restrained by its own internal traditions of constitutional procedure, seemed a much less likely threat to American liberty than the tendencies toward mob rule, enforced conformity, and brutalization which were so pervasive within the individual colonies.

The career and writings of Jonathan Sewall provide one illustration of this Loyalist attitude toward the empire and toward liberty.[6] Sewall is of particular interest because he was a principal participant in the constitutional debate preceding the revolution and then after the war he drafted a plan of government for the remaining British colonies in North America. He was a native of Massachusetts, the fourth generation of his family to live in America. He attended Harvard on scholarship and after graduation in 1718 read law. he became an outstanding trial lawyer. According to his friend, John Adams, Sewall possessed as much power over the minds of a jury "as any lawyer ought to have," and Adams pointedly praised his "lively wit, pleasing humor, brilliant imagination, great subtlety of reasoning and . . . insinuating eloquence."[7]

In 1762, Sewall was made a Justice of the Peace for Middlesex County, and in the following year he published the first in the series of essays which he wrote between 1763 and 1775 in order to defend the policies of the provincial and imperial governments. Sewall's talents as a lawyer and a pamphleteer were duly appreciated by government. In 1767 he became Attorney General of Massachusetts, and in 1769 he was also made Judge of the Vice-Admiralty court for Quebec, Newfoundland, and Nova Scotia, although he arranged, with Governor Hutchinson's blessing, for a substitute to perform the duties of this latter office so that he and his powerful pen could remain in Boston. When the British evacuated Boston, Sewall and his family retired to England to await the restoration of order in America. He enjoyed the London scene enormously and helped to found the Adelphi Club there for Loyalist refugees from New England. He also spent long hours with Thomas Hutchinson and other Loyalist patriarchs planning the Loyalists' triumphant return to America and deciding which offices should go to whom in the postwar colonial establishment. Sewall kept himself informed on the war's progress by corresponding with various Loyalists who had remained in America, and he never lost faith in an ultimate British victory. Thus the government's concession of full independence to the Americans in 1783, and its failure to provide any real protection for the Loyalists in the peace treaty, stunned Sewall so completely that he largely withdrew from public life. He did emerge briefly in 1785 to submit an interesting plan for the government of British North America. Then in 1787, he moved to Saint John, New Brunswick, to take up his appointment to the Council of this new Loyalist province, and to assume his duties as Judge of the Vice-Admiralty Court. At first he seemed rejuvenated by the bustling prosperity of Saint John, but the decision of Great Britain in 1787 to abolish the Court and pension Sewall off renewed his feelings of frustration. Even the receipt of £1600 in claim money could not revive his spirits, and he spent the final years of his life, according to Edward Winslow, "mad at a rascally world because they have not done Justice to his merit."[8]

The question as to why this well-established, unquestionably talented colonial American chose to devote his career to the preservation of British rule in America has received different answers. John Adams and John Hancock attributed his position to a combination of personal pique and greed. As they told it, Sewall was infuriated when the Massachusetts General Court, led by James Otis, refused to pay the debts incurred by his deceased uncle, Chief Justice Stephen Sewall, and he became an easy prey to the blandishments and lucrative offices held out by Francis Bernard and Thomas Hutchinson.[9] There is doubtless some truth in this, just as there is surely some truth in Sewall's judgment that Adams's support of the Revolution was based on "an un-bounded ambition" and that "his zeal for the imagined, or real, glory and welfare of his Country" was the "offspring . . . of disappointed ambition."[10]

Yet however much Sewall enjoyed the prestige and rewards which public service brought him, he was not an uncritical, obse-quious officeholder. Twice during the decade before the Revolu-tion, he risked his public career rather than support a policy which violated his concept of due process of law. In 1768 he incurred the formidable wrath of the Commissioners of Customs by his refusal to prosecute John Hancock, in the case of the *Lydia,* on a bill of information because, in his opinion, such a procedure was novel in the colonies and might be interpreted as a subversion of the defendant's rights in a criminal case.[11] Again, in 1770 Sewall laid himself open to severe censure from both the supporters and the opponents of government, when he refused to participate in the trial of Captain Preston and the soldiers involved in the Boston massacre, because he feared that his own public notoriety would prevent the men from getting a fair trial.[12]

In fact, Sewall's complicated, somewhat vacillating conduct during the 1760s and 1770s suggests what his political writings confirm—that he was primarily interested in the prosperity and harmony of his own particular colony, and that his support of British rule in America grew out of his reflections on the state of American society. Like most denizens of the eighteenth century, Sewall had a fundamentally dark, pessimistic attitude toward human nature. Man in solitary isolation was, in Sewall's opinion, a weak, fallible creature capable of being enslaved by his passions or overwhelmed by the forces of the natural world. It was society which ennobled men, which harnessed their energies in a constructive manner. Through society, men could enjoy the pleasures of human companionship and together tap the riches of the physical universe so that they became, in Sewall's majestic phrase, "the Lords of this lower world."[13] Although Sewall himself believed that "true self love and social love are one and the same thing," he was profoundly aware of man's selfish, anti-social impulses.[14] "For such is the nature of man," he wrote in 1767, "such are the passions and principles implanted in him, that when everyone is left at his natural liberty to do, in all cases, as his inclinations lead him, this is *de facto,* the dissolution of society."[15]

Sewall feared this destructive, passionate side of human nature and he felt that society needed strong bulwarks to protect itself against man's more capricious moments. The most important institution for the preservation of the social order was, in his opinion, the law, "for the law . . . is no respecter of persons; it is founded upon the fix'd basis of right reason; therefore Sir, the Law, Sir, is *semper eadem,* it is permanent, it cannot alter, that is to say, it will not alter to please any, it is not to be trifled with, it is to be honored, it ought not to be blasphemed. . . ."[16] More generally, Sewall felt that the British system of constitutional government was, as he put it, "best adapted to procure to individuals the blessings and advantages of society, and at the same time, to secure to them that Liberty, the loss of which only, can overbalance these advantages."[17]

Beyond these rather familiar bulwarks of the law and the English constitution, Sewall realized that the peaceful existence of a political society depended on the support of the governed. This is not to imply that Sewall was a democrat in any sense; philosophically he was an aristocrat who would have liked to see the more substantial, experienced members of the community given a predominant voice in public affairs. But he was also a good Whig, who recognized that public authority in a free society must ultimately rest on the voluntary consent of the populace. Consequently Sewall's main concern, in the political essays which he wrote between 1763 and 1775, was to reestablish a broad basis of support for government.

Sewall pursued two main themes in his essays. His first and more obvious target was the danger that irresponsible demagogues posed to government and society. He feared that by listening to the harangues of every "bold, disaffected popular declaimer, we are in utmost hazard of raising a tyrant on the ruins of our liberty."[18] Sewall used both personal invective and public ridicule to condemn such critics as James Otis and the New England clergy who, he said, were undermining civil authority by keeping the province in "a continual flame."[19] As early as 1762, Sewall recognized the radical, anti-establishment thrust of these critics and the destructive power of their remarks. Otis and his Junto did not want true liberty, Sewall maintained. Instead they were seeking an unrestrained, absolute kind of freedom: "a liberty, consisting in freedom of speech, freedom of the press, uncontrol'd by the unmanly, slavish tyes [sic] of duty and decency, a liberty to rail at Kings and those in authority, and boldly bid defiance to good government, good breeding, and common sense:—a liberty for every dabbler in politics to say and print whatever his shallow understanding or vicious passions may suggest, against the wisest and best men—a liberty for fools and madmen to spit and throw firebrands at those of the most respectable and amiable characters." In Sewall's opinion, these "Villains . . . who prostitute the sacred names of patriot and liberty to the base, ignoble purposes of vicious passions and licentiousness" were "bold impudent intruders upon the public tranquility."[20]

The fury that gripped Sewall when he discussed these government critics can be explained by the second theme in his essays. This was the danger of utopianism. Sewall feared that his well-meaning countrymen, carried away by an idealistic yet simplistic notion of liberty and virtue, might throw away the social peace and solid traditions of constitutional government which they actually enjoyed in Massachusetts. He was aware of the intoxicating charm of the word liberty.[21] He was also aware of the readiness of the average man to find fault with his fellow man. "However rational the duty of charity and mutual forbearance may appear *in speculation,*" he noted sadly, "the generality of mankind are too prone . . . to form their notions of the character of men, only from the common defects which envy, malice, and revenge may point out."[22] And Sewall recognized that in public life these impulses could be played upon to undermine confidence in public authority. "Whatever tends to create in the minds of the people a contempt of those who hold the highest offices in the state," he declared, "tends to destroy the state itself, because the person and the office are inevitably connected in the people's minds."[23]

To counteract these dangers, Sewall tried in his political writings to restore elements of rationality, perspective, and logic to the public forum. He began with a pragmatic, tough-minded set of premises. All human institutions he declared were liable to corruption and error, just as "all collective bodies of men were composed of good and bad, virtuous and vicious."[24] In man's imperfect state, moreover, it was exceedingly difficult to perceive the truth, "to pervade the mists which passions, party spirit, prejudice, and iniquity have raised."[25] Sewall then proceeded to beg his countrymen to make allowance for these aspects of human fallibility in judging public isues. He was not by any means advocating the doctrine of passive obedience, he assured them. But he did believe in two fundamental propositions: first, that in an admittedly imperfect world, the English form of government was "the wisest and best that has ever appeared *in reality,*" and second, that there was not "a spot on the globe, where public and private justice is administered with a more equal, impartial hand" than in the colony of Massachusetts. This

system could not function, however, if judges and public officials were constantly hounded by "threats or promises of those
in superior power or by the clamours of the populace or the
harangues of Demagogues." Essentially Sewall pled for more
caution, more humility in public life. It was better, he asserted,
to "tolerate small tho' real evils than by an overhasty attempt to
eradicate them, to run the hazard of subverting a good constitution."[26] And he suggested to his countrymen that the British
Parliament—and the King in particular—were far safer guardians
of their liberties than those reckless, self-appointed patriots who
were striking at the very vitals of society by alienating the affec-
tions of the people from all authority.[27]

By 1773, when Sewall entered the political forum for the last
time before the Revolution, his worst fears seem to have been
realized. Passion rather than reason ruled the colony, and the
people, beguiled by "crafty and ambitious demagogues" were no
longer able to discern "who is a Patriot and who is an Enemy to
his country." Sewall tried to view this condition philosophically,
as a "critical season" in the history of Massachusetts when the
minds of men were "peculiarly apt to be agitated and
disturbed." Only time could cure the fever, he felt, could "still
the Tumult of the Passions," and restore the rule of reason to
public affairs.[28] In 1775, soon after the armed struggle began in
Massachusetts, Sewall painted this gloomy picture of those
whom he termed the "Worshippers of Liberty" in his colony:
"Some plunging themselves, their wives and their children in certain poverty and destruction, quitting or wasting their substance,
strolling about like pilgrims, not knowing whither they are
bound; others plundering & destroying all around them . . . the
whole troop rushing into the arms of Slavery and all in honor of
the aforesaid goddess Liberty, as Indians cut and mangle
themselves to please the Devil."[29]

Although Sewall was convinced that the colonists were
deluded rather than vicious, he felt equally certain that only the
application of superior force would bring them to their senses.
And he retired to England while the British army began this
necessary task. The actual course of the war confirmed his worst
fears about the tendency of the revolutionary leaders to override

true personal liberty in pursuit of their utopian goals. When the state of Massachusetts formally banished Sewall in 1778 and confiscated his property, he was enraged—not so much, it would seem, because of the material loss to himself, since he could always look to the British for compensation, but because of the political significance of this act—"To rob and plunder," he said, "and then to banish from their native Country, upon pain of Death, those whose only Crime has been the Exercise of the right of private judgment! to deny the privileges of breathing the common Air to those who have only withdrawn themselves from the horrors and calamities of Civil War!" This, in his opinion, was an "open disregard of common Justice" and the "natural and social rights of Mankind."[30]

It was during his years of exile that Sewall revealed most forcibly his love for his native land and his belief in the potential greatness of North America. He consistently referred to himself as a true patriot and well-wisher to America. And he confidently expected that, in the fullness of time, an independent America would not only be master of the western hemisphere but even of Europe itself.[31] In fact, it was precisely Sewall's faith in the ultimate power and grandeur of America that made him wish to see the colonies continue to develop within the framework of the British empire. His reasons were both positive and negative. The positive reason was his conviction that Great Britain had proven herself to be an agent of liberty and knowledge in the world, and he, of course, wished to see these virtues flourish in North America. The negative reason was Sewall's fear that if Britain should abandon her colonies, their obvious wealth would tempt another foreign power, like France, to come in and conquer them. Then, he gloomily predicted, she would realize "all those grievances under a French master, which she only imagined under a fond indulgent British parent."[32] Sewall's high estimate of America's value also enabled him to remain more optimistic than most Loyalists about the outcome of the war, since he truly felt that Britain could never let these colonies go. Even the shattering news of the defeat at Saratoga did not upset his complacency, and he tried to bolster the spirits of his Loyalist friends with this explanation of the event: ". . . his Majesty, heaven long preserve him, is a great lover of Musick—a Shrewd Sign that in his composition is too much of the *Milk* of human nature, to suffer him to deal *justly* with our damned, fanatical, republican, New England, rebellious, ungenerous, ungrateful sons of bitches! Oh, how I wish they had had for their Sovereign, for a little time, an unfeeling, politic King of Prussia or Empress of Russia . . ."[33] Sewall, of course, regretted the weakness of the British war effort as much as any Loyalist, but he remained confident that they would all meet again in Massachusetts.

The actual success of American independence was, inevitably, intensely disapointing to Sewall. He tried, however, in public to maintain the same air of reasonableness and concern which had characterized his career. He wished his American friends well and formally apologized to any he might have offended in the heat of debate. Yet he could not entirely conceal his forebodings about America's future. To his protégé, Ward Chipman, he confessed that "as matters now stand, I sincerely wish the event may prove that I have been all along mistaken in my Ideas—but I fear America stands upon the brink of inevitable ruin."[34] He advised Chipman to resettle in Halifax rather than expose himself to the permanent instability of a republican government. And he mused, "What form the Wisdom of these new states will finally adopt is beyond the reach of my Judgment or Conjecture. I presume they will not deign to copy from any that has yet existed. Dr. Price's fantastical scheme of *self-government* will be the leading principle with every Man Woman & child throughout the 13 states; & what this can produce time alone can evince— probably 13 or possibly 1300 states, truly anarchical, and this will undoubtedly terminate in absolute *Monarchy*."[35] In another, particularly despondent letter to Chipman, Sewall predicted that the people of America would continue to be led by demagogues, "as if they were a herd of Jack-Asses . . . Poor Beasts, I pity them from my soul—how have their leaders coaxed them on . . . by the empty sounds of Liberty and property, redress of Grievances, the Majesty of the People, Independence! Good God, where is now their Liberty, property, majesty, and Independence. What is the fruit of all their folly but an exchange of imaginary for real and substantial grievances.''[36]

Sewall's last important political act was to draft a plan of government for the remaining British provinces in North America. This was one of a series of proposals drafted by such men as William Smith, jr., William Knox, Benjamin Marston, Edward Winslow and Sir Guy Carleton during the 1780s. Their purpose was not merely to establish stable government in each of the provinces, but to devise a social and political structure which was so wise, so secure, so conducive to good social order and general prosperity, that its obvious superiority would induce the more respectable inhabitants of the American republic to move north. There is a basic similarity among all of these plans and, taken together, they provide a valuable index to Loyalist criticisms of British colonial government before the American Revolution as well as their positive prescriptions for the government of the remaining colonies.

Sewall's plan called for a federal, highly centralized, stratified structure for the government of British North America.[37] At the top of the colonial pyramid there would be a President and a Privy Council, who were to be appointed by the King and drawn from the most substantial, eminent segments of colonial society. This body was given extensive administrative powers over the individual provinces, including the approval of all legislation, regulation of the military forces and the currency and the right to suspend local governors or councillors for misconduct. In effect, Sewall sought to transfer to this federal, supervisory body most of the executive functions of the British government, so that decision making would be both more efficient and more attuned to local needs. Interestingly enough, he gave the native members of the federal Privy Council a good deal of independent power by making it mandatory for the President to consult them on all substantive matters and by having their appointments run during good behavior.

The reforms which Sewall proposed for the government of the individual colonies arose directly from his experience in Massachusetts. Although he felt that the people's right to elect representatives to a legislative assembly went to the very heart of English constituional government, he wished to change the basis of representation by fixing the total number of delegates who could attend the assembly, raising the property qualification, and eliminating the residency requirement. At the level of local government, Sewall felt that it was essential to place firm limits on the number of town meetings which could be held in any one year and on the subjects they could discuss. He also had many suggestions for the judicial and educational institutions in each province, the most important of which were the provision for judges to be appointed at a fixed salary during good behavior, and the recommendation that the heads of public seminaries and colleges should hold religious views which did not "point them decidedly to republicanism." Sewall qualified this last point by noting that he did not wish to make any "illiberal distinctions between different opinions among protestants." In terms of imperial relations Sewall insisted that Parliament must forswear forever the right to tax the colonies, and the colonies must agree to obey the Navigation Acts for a similar length of time. Finally, Sewall felt that all officers of government, heads of colleges and teachers, lawyers and students must take a formal oath of allegiance to the state.

There were many other interesting details in Sewall's plan, but perhaps this summary review will disclose his purpose. In essence, Sewall proposed to substantially increase the amount of executive and legislative power possessed by the colonies and to vest this additional power in the most experienced, loyal members of the community, so as to provide the colonies with a truly responsive system of government and to lay the basis for an equal, harmonious relationship with the empire.

Jonathan Sewall was only one of several Loyalists who tried to devise a new political structure which would give the North American colonies a full, necessary measure of internal self-government and enable them to retain the economic and political benefits of membership in the British empire. The practical application of their ideas can be seen in Lord North's instructions to the Carlisle Commission in 1778, in the specific policies which the Loyalist leaders of New Brunswick tried to implement in their new province, in the Constitutional Act of 1791 which established the governments of Upper and Lower Canada, and in the development of the concepts of responsible government and dominion status. To cite just one example of how these ideas continued from generation to generation, it is noteworthy that Sewall's son, Jonathan Sewall, jr., who served the province of Lower Canada (Quebec) as Chief Justice, President of the Executive Council, and Speaker of the Legislative Council, himself wrote two plans for the federation of the British North American provinces—and that in 1839 one of his last political acts was to present these plans to the visiting Lord Durham.[38] There were, of course, many other elements which contributed to the formulation of the concepts of responsible government and dominion status. But the dream of a voluntary, co-operative, politically homogenous empire, which was spawned in America in the 1750s, continued to inspire both British and colonial political figures until it achieved its final embodiment in the British Commonwealth of nations.

The history of this imperial ideal—so different from the imperialism of the late nineteenth and twentieth centuries—has not yet been traced in any comprehensive fashion. Yet surely this— rather than the American Revolution *per se*—is the proper frame of reference for understanding Loyalist history. So long as the Loyalists are seen solely within the framework of the American Revolution, even the most sympathetic, fair-minded historian must conclude that they were "losers"—admirable personally perhaps, but losers politically. For the context of the debate over the American Revolution, taken in isolation, does make the Loyalists appear to be men out of joint with their time, men who resisted the "wave of the future" in order to cling to a secure, comfortable present.

If, on the other hand, the Loyalists are viewed in the context of the Anglo-American empire described here, with its own separate but no less noble vision of the future of the North American continent, then a more positive view of their role and accomplishments is possible. It is here that the political writings of men like Jonathan Sewall, the numerous plans for the reorganization of the colonies both before and after the Revolution, and the actual policies which the Loyalists pursued in governing the provinces of British North America are particularly instructive. Taken as a piece, these measures enable us to comprehend the totality of the Loyalist experience. And they suggest that by pursuing the Loyalists after the war, into Canada and the British imperial service, we will discover that these men were not out of tune with their times, but rather that they were marching to a different drummer. The Loyalists clearly shared the common American belief in the rich potential of their young continent. Yet they also recognized the disruptive, levelling tendencies in American life, and the feared that, without the British "sheet anchor" to keep the colonies on course, liberty might turn into license, popularity might replace merit as the standard for public reward, excellence might give way to personal gratification, and the incipient violence which always lurked below the surface of eighteenth century American society might break through the thin tissue of restraint which the colonists had managed to erect. The Loyalist effort to preserve British rule in North America was the result of their profound commitment to personal liberty, social order, and a civilized quality of life. When the thirteen colonies determined to break completely with Great Britain, the Loyalists carried their political and social goals with them to their new homes in British North America and planted them deep in the Canadian heritage. By relating Loyalist history to this dream of an Anglo-American empire, it is possible to view their experience before and after the war as a single entity and to see these men for what they were— bold, imaginative, committed participants in the development of North American society.

TRIBAL LOYALTY

AND

TRIBAL INDEPENDENCE

BY

FRANCIS JENNINGS

===========

IN approaching the role played by Indian tribes in the American Revolution, a historian must first demythologize his conceptions. Three kinds of myth cloud this field: the myth of Indian savagery, the myth of British sovereignty, and the myth of colonial libertarianism.

For present purposes the most pertinent aspects of the myth of savagery reflect notions of government and territory. The first invading European colonizers of America decided that Indians were wild and licentious, not only lacking in civil government, but incapable by nature of becoming civilized. In their various languages all the colonizers called the natives "wild men." The English picked up the French version *saulvage* (derived from the Latin *silva*, meaning woods), and the English considered those *savages* to be roaming people of the wilderness rather than people settled in villages and towns. Englishmen were very explicit about what such wildness implied. To them it meant that the Indians had no government worthy of the name. The corollary became a religious obligation for Englishmen to give a proper civil government to those savages, even when the benighted ones irrationally opposed that boon.

There were other implications, equally significant, expressed in purest form by the chronicler Samuel Purchas. The barbarians, he wrote, "having not the Law, were a law to themselves." They were "not worthy of the name of a Nation, being wilde and Savage." So bad a people, "having little of Humanitie but shape, ignorant of Civilitie, of Arts, of Religion; more brutish than the beasts they hunt, more wild and unmanly than that unmanned wild Countrey, which they range rather than inhabite . . . hence have wee fit objects of zeale and pitie, to deliver from the power of darkness." In recompense, "all the rich endowments of Virginia, her Virgin-portion from the creation nothing lessened, are wages for all this worke: God in wisedome having enriched the Savage Countries, that those riches might be attractives for Christian suters, which there may sowe spirituals and reape temporals."[1] Though the language is on the lurid side, the point is clear: since the Indians had neither government nor religion, and just wandered about over the land, that "unmaned" land was free to be taken. Indeed, duty demanded that Christian English gentlemen should seize it and the Indians for their own good.

We must not too readily commit the error of thinking that Purchas really believed everything he wrote. He was engaged in a project of justification and rationalization of the conduct of the Virginia Company of London which had been ungratefully resisted by the "unnatural naturals" of Virginia. Purchas knew very well that the Indians of Virginia lived in sedentary villages and cultivated the land. He knew that they lived under governments of chiefs and councils and had precedent-established customs that were enforced as rigorously as the precedent-established common law of England. He was well-acquainted with these facts from the same sources in which we find them today, the writings of his friend Captain John Smith and other Virginia colonists. But his job was to create an image of those Indians that would make them morally deserving of conquest and subjection, and he pursued that object without regard to facts.

I have spent so much time with Purchas because features of his fiction were to become established in popular imagination, to be repeated even into the twentieth century, and for the same reason he held originally; namely, to justify dispossession and subjugation of the Indians. But the eighteenth-century gentlemen who held important offices under the British crown had different understandings, and if we are to clarify for ourselves what went on during the American Revolution we must separate the realism of the statesmen from the ranting of the propagandists.

In regard to Indian government and territory, for instance, General Thomas Gage was gratifyingly explicit in a letter of 7 October 1772 to the Superintendent of Indian Affairs, Sir William Johnson. "It is asserted as a general Principle," wrote Gage, "that the Six [Iroquois] Nations having conquered such and such Nations, their Territories belong to them, and the Six Nations being the Kings Subjects which by treaty they have acknowledged themselves to be, those Lands belong to the King. I believe it is for our Interest to lay down such principles especially when we were squabbling with the French about Territory, and they played us off in the same style of their Indian subjects, and the right of those Indians. . . . If we are to search for truth and examine her to the Bottom, I dont imagine we shall find that any conquered [Indian] Nation ever formally ceded their Country to their Conquerors, or that the latter ever required it . . . As for the Six Nations having acknowledged themselves Subjects of the English, that I conclude must be a very gross Mistake and am well satisfied were they told so, they would not be well pleased."[2]

In consideration of such remarks it should be evident that a prudent historian will follow the informed advice of a former Attorney General of the United States, the insightful John Mitchell: one should pay more attention to what the gentlemen did than to what they said.

The myth of savagery was interwoven with the legal fiction of sovereignty. I can make no comment which would improve upon that of Sir William Johnson. In a private letter to Attorney General John Tabor Kempe of New York dated 7 October 1765, Johnson explicated the discrepancy between the facts and the claims of sovereignty.

. . . it is the policy of our Constitution that Whereso-ever the Kings Dominions extend, he is the fountain of all property in Lands &c. But how can this be made to Extend to the native rights of a people whose property none of our Kings have claimed a right to invade, & to whom the Laws have never Extended without which Dominion canot be said to be Exercised.

Strictly speaking our rights of Soil Extend no farther than they are actually purchased by Consent of the Natives, 'tho' in a political Sense our Claims are much more Extensive, & in several Colonies include Lands we never saw, and over which we could not Exercise full Dominion with 10,000 of the best Troops in Europe, but these Claims are kept up by European powers to prevent the Encroachments or pretensions of each other, nor can it be consistent with the Justice of our Constitution to extend it farther in this Case.

These Extensive Claims had their Origin from the practice of the Popes who took upon them to give away all Countrys not Christian in favour of Some Sons of the Church whose Clergy & Subjects were to Convert them, but in reality to deprive them of their Possessions, Libertys, and Lives. This induced our Kings to take upon themselves Similar rights, & their Adventurers took possesion of several places in the Language of the times by Setting up Crosses &c. After them Succeeding Adventurers purchased & Effected Settlements on the Sea Coasts from the Natives and afterwards in the same manner made Gradual advances into the Interior parts of this Continent. Which was the Case of this Province [New York] in particular, no Conquest having been made, nor any Indian Transactions tending to more than that of putting their Lands under the protection of the Crown, to prevent the fraudulent Dealings they had often Experienced, but the right of Soil always remained to the Indians & in this Sense it has always been considered by our Monarchs as will appear from the Steps to be taken for acquiring a property in America by Deed from the Natives whose title is indisputable,

and who are therein declared to have good right &
full power to dispose thereof as Expressed in their
Grants.[3]

So much for sovereignty.

Finally we must consider the myth that the American Revolutionaries fought for liberty. Its durability is to be explained by a
partial substance of truth. The Revolutionaries did indeed struggle for their own liberties, but as has often been noted they were
not eager to extend those liberties to persons of darker complex-
ion. So far as Indians were concerned, the very clear objective of
the states seceding from the British empire was to create an
empire of their own by subjugating and dispossessing the western
tribes. Through the Royal Proclamation of 1763 and the Quebec
Act of 1774 the British government had deprived its colonists of
the liberty of seizing and occupying tribal territories; to recover
that liberty the colonists had to destroy the crown's power to
protect the Indians.

Certainly there were other issues between crown and colonies,
but this is the one relevant to our present concern. Because of it,
most Indians became Loyalists in appearance, and the appearance was gruesome enough to their enemies, but it would be a
great mistake for us to conclude that the warriors who served
under British officers were fighting for British rule. They fought
rather to restore British protection for their autonomous tribal
governments and lands. In short, they were fighting against the
colonists rather than for the crown.

Contemporary statesmen—particularly the Superintendents of
Indian Affairs and the members of the Board of Trade—
understood this distinction well, and acted upon it pragmatically
and efficiently, but the myths of savagery, sovereignty, and liberty have hidden it from historians. We have no trouble
distinguishing the separate purposes of the French, Spanish, and
Dutch allies of the colonists, who fought against Britain rather
than for the United States, but we see the Indians only as
"auxiliaries"—something like Hessian mercenaries—and we
therefore are unable to see tribal governments deciding and acting upon policies of their own.

The crown's officers have provided copious evidence that in this respect, at least, they were far from being the muddleheaded dimwits so often portrayed in American histories. Their failures derived less from stupidity in administration than from intractable relationships of real power. They were in a no-win situation. They could keep the formal allegiance of their colonies only by abdicating to the colonies the power of determining the policies of empire.

The particular imperial issue at stake was the disposal of the American lands west of the Appalachian mountain range. In the middle of the eighteenth century this vast territory became an arena of struggle as two great empires and a number of lesser powers disputed its possession. France and Britain came at last to the fated clash that had been in the making ever since they had respectively founded Quebec and Jamestown, and their great contest produced one of the earliest worldwide wars. What must also be taken into account is that Britain's colonies struggled among themselves, politically rather than by force of arms, over the particular jurisdiction each was to exert. Virginia and Pennsylvania laid claim, by charter right, to the same lands in the region where Pittsburgh now stands, and their leading officials (who were generally also their leading land speculators) conspired deeply against each other at the same time they all fought the French.[4] One of the conspirators was young George Washington who suffered a rebuke from British General John Forbes in 1758 for clandestinely trying to divert the general's military road from Pennsylvania to Virginia.[5] Within the colonies, pro- and anti-imperialist factions foreshadowed the future as they struggled over provision of funds to support the war; there was no universal patriotic surge forward to pay taxes. Finally, there were the Indian tribes who claimed the land as their own, but even they were at odds with each other about precisely which tribe had the genuine right of jurisdiction at particular places; for example, the mixed tribes in occupation along the Allegheny and Ohio rivers claimed the territory as their own, but the Iroquois Six Nations laid a claim to hegemony from their homeland in the Finger Lakes region of New York.[6]

As a consequence the Seven Years War in America was not a

simple affair, and it decided nothing except the elimination of France. The other struggles continued and grew more intense. Indian resentment came to crisis immediately after British troops moved in to occupy Indian territories. Historians have prejudiced what ensued by scornfully naming it "Pontiac's Conspiracy," but it was in fact a giant system of tribal alliances that laid siege to British forts in the most widespread war for Indian independence that Britain had ever faced.[7] Though we have read much of Indian atrocities in that war, perhaps we might remember that General Sir Jeffrey Amherst broke the siege of Fort Pitt by ordering its garrison to infect the Indian besiegers with smallpox; this was done, and the epidemic that followed gave victory to the upholders of "civilization."[8]

The tribes were defeated but not conquered. The sieges were lifted and peace treaties were negotiated, but the warriors were still at large and still capable of wreaking immense havoc if pushed to desperation. The crown was precariously deep in debt after the long war with France, and ministers could not consider another long and expensive war of Indian conquest as a tolerable option. They tried instead to pacify the Indians by alleviating their grievances, and thus drew down upon the ministers' own heads the wrath of the colonists who were the source of the Indians' grievances. As the French had formerly ordered Virginians to stay out of the west, so now the British crown did the same thing by issuing the Royal Proclamation of 1763 which defined the Indian territories as reserved crown lands and forbade the colonists to settle there. It did not matter to the colonists that the rationale of the British government differed from that previously uttered by the French; the Virginians perceived only that the end results were the same. The lucrative expansion formerly prohibited by the French crown was now prohibited by the British, and the hostility formerly directed toward Paris was soon transferred to London.

An immediate explosion over this issue was postponed, however, by distractions and mitigating circumstances. The chief distraction was an explosion over a different issue, the Stamp Act of 1765. This is so well known as to need little comment, but we may notice that it was not an effort to pay off the debts

of the Seven Years War, as is so often alleged, but rather an
expedient to pay the current costs of garrisoning the western Indian country. The subsequent repeal of the Stamp Tax did
nothing to lighten that continuing burden, and the ministry was
left with a dilemma. Either the troops had to be withdrawn to
prevent bankruptcy, in which case the probability of vast and
prolonged Indian wars seemed strong, or other means of defray-
ing the expense of the troops had to be devised, in which case
the ministry faced the necessity of choosing between two evils: it
might commit political suicide by taxing Englishmen still more
heavily to support troops protecting Americans, or it might incur
the renewed wrath of the American colonists by taxing them to
pay for garrisons enforcing the ban on colonial expansion into
Indian territory. None of these options were desirable, but
British statesmen could not remain in doubt as to which of the
evils must be endured. The troops stayed, and the colonists were
taxed.[9]

The colonists displayed considerable ingratitude for the
crown's kindly care. There were broils and riots. The Government moved, as government must, to restore order. The effort
required troops. As crises worsened, troops were withdrawn
from garrisons in the western wilderness to go into garrison in
the eastern towns. Swiftly, the taxes to pay for an army to pacify
Indians became taxes used for an army to pacify colonials. The
transformation did not improve colonial dispositions, and there
was more violence until the ministry resorted to the Coercive
Acts of 1774 to make an example of Boston. At this point,
however, Whitehall did make a serious miscalculation that rallied
powerful land speculators in Virginia and Pennsylvania to
Boston's support. Shortly after passing the Coercive Acts, Parliament passed the Quebec Act also, and thereby brought to boil
a ferment that had been working since 1763. The colonials
lumped the Quebec Act in with the Coercive Acts, calling them
all Intolerable Acts, and their governments turned a united face
against Britain. Whitehall had had good political and moral
grounds for wanting the Quebec Act, but its timing was
disastrously bad. We must backtrack to see how this policy
evolved.

The crown had first become deeply concerned about Indians at the beginning of the Seven Years War with France. Until that time each colony negotiated Indian treaties separately in its own interest, which often conflicted with the interests of other colonies, and the treaties were sometimes fraudulent, sometimes agreed to by the Indians under duress. Indian grievances accumulated, especially with regard to colonial seizures of tribal territories, and as hostilities with France began the British government faced the dire possibility of having to fight French and Indian allies without allies of their own. The Board of Trade summoned an interprovincial congress at Albany in 1754 to rectify the situation.[10]

The Albany congress has been much touted for its plan of provincial union, so prominently associated with Benjamin Franklin's name, but the plan was rejected on all sides and the congress demonstrated the very opposite of unity. In consequence, the Board of Trade recognized that Indian relations were degenerating into chaos under provincial management and it moved to take them under the crown's direct supervision. Two new officers were appointed: the Superintendents of Indian Affairs for the Northern and Southern Districts. They primarily had military functions at first; their jobs were to recruit Indian allies in the war. In this they succeeded, but the price of success was a solemn pledge on behalf of the crown to protect the tribes in their territorial rights.[11]

By 1763 the Indians came to believe that this pledge had been violated, that they had been betrayed; and they rose, as already remarked, in the war for liberation named after Pontiac. While General Amherst used military means to suppress that rising, the statesmen at Whitehall used a political approach through the Royal Proclamation of 1763. This laid down a barrier line across the top of the Apalachians, and forbade colonial settlement to the west. In doing this the crown rescinded the territorial provisions of a number of colonial charters that provided for boundaries extending from the Atlantic Ocean to the Pacific.[12]   We have already seen Sir William Johnson's interpretation of the value of those charters, but the reaction was especially strong in Virginia. It had been the western adventuring of the Ohio Company of Virginia that precipitated the war with France, and the Virginians' rough treatment was a primary cause of Indian disaffection. (The Indian name for a Virginian was "Big Knife," and it was not a compliment.) When the British crown laid down its Proclamation barrier line, it reduced to zero the value of the huge investments made by Virginians in the Ohio region. It is noteworthy that one of the families most heavily involved in those investments was that of George Washington. So also was the family of Richard Henry Lee who was to argue in Congress for the independence of the United States.[13]

In 1763 there was still a possibility that the losses could be recovered through a legal maneuver. Though the Proclamation line put a western limit to the old seaboard colonies, it did not preclude the possibility of new colonial jurisdiction beyond the line. It was, after all, merely a royal administrative decree and it could be revoked or modified by royal issuance of new charters. The speculators and their lobbyists swarmed over London with vast schemes to convert the western crown lands (i.e., the Indian territories) into new chartered colonies, and from 1763 to 1774 the situation remained fluid.[14]

The Board of Trade, however, had taken its Indian policies seriously. In a most remarkable document circulated to colonial officials in 1764 it suggested a scheme for regulation of the tribes that was strongly reminiscent of feudal times. In this plan the royal Superintendents of Indian Affairs would become, in effect, great lords protector over the tribes with retinues of hired employees to supervise trade. The tribes would continue to be formally self-governing, but would elect chiefs to serve in a capacity very like vassalage. It was, in short, a plan of government transition from tribe to state. But it was expensive, and it was dropped.[15]

While statesmen and speculators waltzed in London, the tribes threatened to begin the war dance in the west. Squatters were ignoring the Proclamation line and pouring unchecked into tribal lands.[16] As the threat of war mounted, the crises within the colonies simultaneously multiplied, and the ministry had to decide whether to make concessions to the colonies while repressing the Indians or to make concessions to the Indians while repressing the colonies. There could be no further concessions to the colonies without passing the point of no return. On the other hand, the Indians could be mollified only by making them genuinely secure, at least for a season, against further colonial expansion. From such circumstances the boundary provisions of the Quebec Act followed logically.

The primary purpose of the Quebec Act was to establish a permanent civil government for the Canadian lands ceded by France after the Seven Years War, but the Act provided also that one of Quebec's boundaries should run down to the Ohio River along the line that had been set by the Royal Proclamation of 1763. Frenchmen already living in scattered settlements west of that line would be under Quebec's government, but Indians would continue to live tribally under the general protection of the Superintendent of Indian Affairs for the Northern District. The old Board of Trade plan was revised to be used as a guide for the regulation of the Indian trade.[17]

The Quebec Act was a much stronger instrument of policy than the Royal Proclamation. Whereas the Proclamation was subject to administrative rescission at any time, an Act of Parliament could only be undone by another Act of Parliament. And whereas the squatters in Indian territory had been ignored or encouraged by colonial authorities, the Governor of Quebec would enforce his bounds and had troops directly under his command. Above all, no patents to real property could be issued without his approval and he was remote from the influence of colonial speculators. Thee factors explain why the Act's passage caused the speculator lobbyists, who had previously been professing devout loyalty to the crown, to return from London to assume leading roles in the revolutionary movement.[18]

The Continental Congress understood the Quebec Act's implications so well that it organized an invasion of Canada almost a full year before it declared independence. If the west was to belong to Canada, the Congressmen were determined that Canada would belong to them. The Canadians thought otherwise, however, and the invaders returned empty-handed.[19]

When hostilities between crown and colonies broke out, Indian allies were solicited by both sides while each side denounced the other and denied its own involvement in such dirty doings. For the most part, the Indians themselves tried at first to stay clear of the war, but when that effort failed the bulk of them fought against the colonial encroachers on their lands. They never for a moment relinquished the right to dispose of those lands. Their surprise was great, therefore, when they heard at the end of the colonists' war with Britain that the United States had acquired their lands by the Treaty of Paris in 1783.[20]

Knowing as we do how the British privately regarded their claim to sovereignty, it seems likely that they assumed the United States would receive it with the same understanding; namely, that it was a fence against intrusion by European powers, but not a pen enclosing Indians. The Americans, however, chose to magnify sovereignty to a conception they themselves had never tolerated while their sovereign was the King of Great Britain. At the Treaty of Fort Stanwix in 1784 commissioners of the United States informed chiefs of the Iroquois Six Nations that the Indians had lost all territorial rights through conquest.[21] There was an acute difference of opinion. Separate commissioners from Pennsylvania tacitly disregarded this bombast and carefully negotiated a purchase of yet-unceded Indian territories as far as the limit of Pennsylvania's claimed boundaries.[2] The western tribes proved that they had not been conquered by taking up the hatchet once more and continuing at war for another ten years. They were finally defeated in the Battle of Fallen Timbers, but by the time they negotiated peace at the Treaty of Greenville in 1795 they had convinced the government of the United States that the previous British conception of sovereignty was correct. Just as at the end of Pontiac's War, the tribes were beaten but not conquered. At Greenville their territorial boundaries were recognized by the United States and when their lands were desired by that government at future times, an act of cession was negotiated by treaty just as had been done previously by the crown.

That these treaties were sometimes fraudulent and sometimes accepted under duress was also in the old pattern. Regardless of that, the legal theory of conquest right was abandoned, and a formal recognition of "Indian title" to lands became so well established in law that the tribes are still collecting compensation in the United States Court of Claims to the extent of hundreds of millions of dollars. If it is true that the crown abandoned its loyal tribes at the Treaty of Paris, it is also true that with their own resources the western tribes compelled the United States government to assume the formal role of the crown—the role of protector rather than ruler—and to confine itself to that role for nearly another hundred years.[23]

FIRST AMERICANS AND LAST LOYALISTS: AN INDIAN DILEMMA IN WAR AND PEACE

BY

PETER MARSHALL

A definition of the Indian role in the revolutionary conflict is far from easy to provide: a few spectacular episodes such as, on the one hand, the Patriot expedition of 1776 against the Cherokees and Sullivan's devastation of the Six Nations' villages in 1779, and on the other, the Wyoming and Cherry Valley massacres, have served to establish a general impression of crimes and punishments, committed and inflicted as a barbaric addendum to the customary limited engagements of eighteenth-century warfare. Tactically, a strong case can be made for the view that the horror aroused by Indian participation in military campaigns far exceeded the assistance thus secured by either side: in any event neither the British nor the American military commanders hastened to bring the tribes into alliance. So Jack Sosin qualifies his judgement that "to Gage belongs the major blame for exaggerating the involvement on the patriot side and encouraging the wide-scale employment of the savages," by the observation that "Carleton and John Stuart did not initially follow his orders and the settlers were thus given two years to prepare."[1] This tardy inclusion of the Indians in the war provides whatever justification can be offered for their total exclusion from the provisions of the Peace. Indian sovereignty, whether proclaimed in terms of wartime alliances or on occasions of the yielding of territory, represented a curiously elusive and flexible concept. On that account there would seem a certain appropriateness in the fate of Benjamin West's composition portraying the "Reception of the American Loyalists by Great Britain": the refugees thus depicted included an Indian chief and the original painting has been lost.[2]

This makes for a readiness to accept Wallace Brown's conclusion that "the Indians are a very special kind of Loyalist," even if his judgement that their distinction was one of "simply following self-interest" appears somewhat too terse an explanation.[3] It does, however, escape the difficulty posed by the more general grounds on which Indians are rendered eligible for consideration in Robert Calhoon's recent study. "To the extent that a large portion of the Iroquois nation [sic] looked on the Crown as protector and benefactor and fought for the British in the War for Independence out of moral obligation as well as self-interest, these Indians were loyalists and subjects as well as independent military allies."[4] So seemingly reasonable a statement in fact muddies, where it does not skirt, the central question: was it possible to be both loyal subject and faithful ally? Even if one accepts the possibility of assigning the proportions of moral obligation and of self-interest contained within Indian attitudes, recourse must be had to the record of events for evidence of whether the British authorities treated Indians as Loyalists or as allies. Such an investigation will extend far further in time than might be anticipated, and requires reference to events occurring long after the fate of the other migrants from the United States had been finally resolved.

At the end of an unsuccessful war the disposal by the vanquished of their auxiliaries presents special difficulties and embarrassments. In some parts of the extensive perimeter of this conflict the problem was comparatively simple to resolve: in the West, tribes could be abandoned without any immediate consequence; on the border between New England and the Maritimes small populations of Indians and settlers, coupled with large distances, provided room for disengagement. Two areas, however, did not offer easy solutions: both had been the scene of bloody conflicts during the war, and in neither case could the

Indians either reconcile themselves to, or withdraw from contact with, the new power that had replaced their former imperial connection. In Florida and New York the Indians could not be locally ignored as they had been during the making of the peace in France.

Indians had played a costly but indecisive part in the Revolutionary war in the South. A recent study has estimated that between 1775 and 1783 British expenditures on Indian affairs in these colonies amounted to some £250,000.[5] The value received in return was disappointing:

> Despite repeated assurances from the Indians of their undying loyalty and their willingness to act in the king's cause, despite expenditures and assiduous labor by the officials of the British Indian Department, the natives never rendered the service expected of them. The only time that the warriors made a substantial contribution came in 1780 when the Creeks and Choctaw aided in the defense of Pensacola against the Spanish . . .[6]

War in the Lower South, though marked by bitter episodes, had proved spasmodic: major conflict did not commence until early 1779 and had drawn to a close by the end of 1781. In the following year a systematic British withdrawal became evident: Savannah was evacuated in July and Charleston in December 1782.

The troops were accompanied by a large number of refugees: by the end of 1782 over 6,000 whites and blacks had been received in East Florida from Georgia and South Carolina. The simultaneous arrival of Indians placed the supplies of the colony under severe strain. Governor Tonyn informed the Commander-in-chief "of the Indians, who have lately come into this province, Creeks, Choctaws, and Cherokees, and sundry nations from the North, Mowhawkes, Senacas, Delawares, Shaneses, Manjoes, Tuscaroras, Yatancus, and other tribes from Fort Detroit . . ." "Your Excellency is sensible this province is not equal to so large a demand of supplies," the harassed Governor concluded, "and that there is no other channel of communication but this province between the southern Indians and the

King's troops.''[7] It was the turn of the Indians to be alarmed with their subsequent discovery that East Florida was to be returned to Spain: this news was officially announced in the colony in April 1783, bringing to a sudden stop the land and population boom created by the arrival of loyal refugees from the southern states.[8]

Thomas Brown, Superintendent of Indian Affairs in East Florida after the death in March 1799 of John Stuart, was particularly disturbed when he received warning of the cession. He feared for the safety of persons and property in the colony when the peace terms became known to the Cherokees and, especially, to the Creeks. Brown's sympathies for that tribe were undisguised. "The situation of our poor unfortunate allies," he wrote to Carleton, "most sensibly affects me. They were ever faithful to me; I never deceived them. Your excellency, I hope, will pardon the liberty of saying, I now feel for my own honor."[9] His feelings were shared by the military commander in St Augustine, Brigadier McArthur, who wrote, the following month, to Carleton expressing his concern at the prospects for Indian relations:

> In all transactions with the Indians I shall consult with the Governor and Superintendant, and use every possible means to conciliate their good will. The minds of these people appear as much agitated as those of the unhappy loyalists on the eve of a third evacuation; and however chimerical it may appear to us, they have very seriously proposed to abandon their country and accompany us, having made all the world their enemies by their attachment to us . . .[10]

A little later Brown reported that he had received a visit from the Creek head warrior, who had declared that his tribe intended to leave with the English forces. Vessels were requested for this purpose.[11] Carleton was sufficiently impressed to respond, grudgingly granting permission for the Indians' removal should they insist on departure. He instructed McArthur that

such of the Indians as persevere in their demand of
being carried to the Bahamas shall be furnished with
the means, but as it is a situation ill-adapted to their
mode of life, and of which they would be soon tired,
you cannot use too many arguments to dissuade them
from a measure destructive of their happiness . . .[12]

Although McArthur subsequently held out hopes that he
would be able to convince the Indians of the disastrous consequences should they leave the country, he evidently failed to convince the Indian Superintendant, since in September Carleton
was informed that ". . . Colonel Brown with a high proportion
of the men and officers of his regiment intends settling in some
of the Bahama Islands . . . he apprehends many of his Indian
friends will insist on accompanying him . . ."[13] Brown, with
members of his regiment, the King's Rangers, withdrew to the
Bahamas, but there is no record of Indians preferring exile to
abandonment.[14] The return of East Florida to Spain offered the
Creeks both the possibility and necessity of reverting to a policy
of self-preservation by playing off Spanish against American
interest: Alexander McGillivray, the undeniable if nominally
unexpected leader of the Creeks, claimed to have taken the first
steps in that direction before the formal end of hostilities. He
reminded Governor Miro:

Some time before the General Peace, when there was
a probability that America would be declared Independent & East & West Florida ceded to the Crown of
Spain, I applied in behalf of the Creek Nation to
Governor O'Neil at Pensacola & offer'd to put the
Creek Nation under his Most Catholic Majestys Protection, as the Americans pretend that we are in their
Boundary. If the British Nation has been Compell'd
to Withdraw its protection from us, She has no right
to give up a Country she never could call her own.
Therefore as a free Nation we have an undoubted
right to chuse what Protection we think proper . . .

McGillivray wasted no time in stressing the fact to the new Governor that if the Spanish did not act quickly the Americans would, of necessity, engross the Indian trade. He explained his authority for so saying:

> It is necessary for me to Inform you that I am a Native of this Nation & of rank in it. At the commencement of the American Rebellion, I entered into the British Service & after a long Contest of faithfull Services we have at the Close been most Shamefully deserted as well as every other people that has relied on their honor & Fidelity . . .[15]

Whites and Blacks, Loyalists and slaves, had departed from Florida rather than return to the United States or submit to Spanish rule. The Indians, though they had threatened to join the exodus, and had certainly induced much alarm among British officials in the last months before the completion of evacuation, preferred in the end to regard themselves as faithful allies betrayed by false friends: their lands were their own and would, if their strength and skill permitted, remain in their hands. It was an old game for new players.

The situation of the Northern Indians resembled, in one respect, that in the South: the Iroquois could attempt to maintain a separate existence by preserving a balance between British and Ameircan, as once they had veered between a British and a French alliance. But the Northern situation was far more complex than that to be found in the South. Although only two tribes, the Mohawks in the North, the Chickasaws in the South,[16] had been steadfast allies of the British, the pursuit of Indian self-interest demanded differing responses in the comparable yet distinctive situations fostered by the coming of peace to Florida and New York. Whereas evacuation enabled Britain to terminate relations with the Southern tribes, in the northern sphere a breaking of relations was neither possible nor desirable. Here, the need of an Indian alliance remained obvious even if their reception as loyal subjects had received no attention from the King and his ministers.

Military and Indian affairs officers in the north greatly feared the reaction of the tribes to a treaty which had been signed without any prior consultation having taken place with them. In Quebec, General Frederick Haldimand, the governor and commander-in-chief, became the most senior official to remind the ministry of its ommission and to issue warnings of the consequences likely to follow from a neglect of the Indians. By late April 1783 Haldimand knew, and the Indians suspected, that the terms of Peace had ignored their interests. In the following month officers at important posts such as Niagara, where numbers of Indians had gathered, were reporting widespread uneasiness at unconfirmed reports of new boundaries "to which they never can agree if true, but they do not believe it." Brigadier Maclean had

> every Reason to believe the Six Nations will act as they have hitherto done, with fidelity, firmness, and moderation; at least while we remain here; but I would by no means answer for what they may do, when they See us Evacuate these Posts. I would rather then be apprehensive of some disagreeable Scenes . . .

Meanwhile, the chiefs of the Six Nations, angered by reports that General Schuyler predicted their destruction by the Americans, had declared that the King had no right to cede lands which were not his to grant. The chiefs had declared

> that the Indians were a free People Subject to no Power upon Earth, that they were the faithful Allies of the King of England but not his Subjects—that he had no right Whatever to grant away to the States of America, their Rights or properties without a manifest breach of all justice and Equity, and they would not Submit to it . . .[17]

Even before this dispatch had reached him, Haldimand had been challenged personally by Joseph Brant to put an end to uncertainty and prove that Britain was grateful for Indian loyalty. "I am now sent," Brant declared in the city of Quebec,

> in behalf of all the King's Indian Allies to receive a decisive answer from you, and to know whether they are included in the Treaty with the Americans, as faithful Allies should be or not, and whether those Lands which the Great Being above has pointed out for Our Ancestors, and their descendants, and Placed them there from the beginning and where the Bones of our forefathers are laid, is secure to them, or whether the Blood of their Grand Children is to be mingled with their Bones, thro' the means of our Allies for whom we have so often so freely Bled . . .[18]

At this juncture the sentiments and aims of Brant and McGillivray appeared to be identical.

The experiences of the tribes during the Revolution, and the affect of the conflict upon them did not, however, sustain the similarity. The Iroquois, it is true, had not hastened to support the British war effort: only in 1777 did any tribe of the Six Nations take an active part in offensive operations.[19] Although a majority had tended to favour their former allies, a sufficient number were prepared to remain friendly towards the Americans to delay an outright declaration of allegiance.[20] The strength, geographical situation, and previous connections of the Iroquois demanded that every effort be made by their British connections to secure their removal from a position of neutrality to one of commitment against the rebels. The principal means by which this change could be brought about involved recourse to the connections—white, red, and half-breed—of the Johnson family. The most important of the Indian elements of this Mohawk valley interest were undoubtedly Molly Brant, housekeeper to the late Superintendent of Indian Affairs and mother of at least nine of his children, and her younger brother Joseph. From the beginning of hostilities no effort was spared to build support for the Crown upon a continued alliance with the Iroquois. So in August 1775 Guy Johnson, nephew and successor of Sir William as Superintendent, his family and Indian department colleagues, with 120 warriors and chiefs of the Six Nations, set out for Montreal, where Governor Carleton received them in conference.[21] Joseph Brant, who formed one of the party, received a captain's commission, and later claimed that full compensation for losses had been promised if they would fight with the British. The Indians were told that

> the war has commenced. Assist the King now, and you will find it to your advantage. Go now and fight for your possessions, and whatever you lose of your property during the war, the King will make up to you when peace returns . . .[2]

Although a confusion of details does not bear out Brant's claim in old age that "since the year 1760, I perfectly remember what has passed at most councils,"[23] he asserted on more than one occasion that Carleton had promised the Indians "should we not prove successful in the contest, that he would put us on the same footing in which we stood previous to our joining him." This pledge, Brant claimed, had been renewed in April 1779 by his successor, Haldimand.[24] These commitments, if entered upon, were undertaken by field commanders and local representatives of the Crown: there is no indication that they represented imperial policy. The consequence of the contest for alliance with the Six Nations between British and Americans was the destruction of the Confederacy: if the battle of Oriskany, fought in August 1777, is taken to mark the beginning of an Indian civil war, the process of disruption appeared complete by the beginning of 1779. Against the pro-British Mohawks could be set the Oneidas and Tuscaroras, who had become friends of the Americans; the Onondagas perhaps best expressed in their attitudes the Iroquois dilemma, being divided into pro-British, pro-American and neutral factions.[25]

Once begun, the conflict raged without either side securing the upper hand. Only an equality of destruction was achieved. The American expeditions of the late summer of 1779 on the New York and Pennsylvania frontiers laid waste Indian lands without crushing their occupants. In the following year the British and their allies killed or captured over three hundred Americans in raids of a comparably devastating scale which ravaged the Mohawk settlements to within a short distance of Albany and Schenectady. The tribes were sufficiently impressed by the experience of 1779 to refuse to move from their new villages west of the Genesee. Henceforth, they did not wish to stray too far from the defences and supplies of Fort Niagara.[26]

By the autumn of 1782 British policy, both in Florida and in Quebec, involved the withdrawal of Indians from situations of potential conflict. In both regions the officers responsible for implementing this decision feaed the reactions of allies who might well construe the change as an act of betrayal.[27] Whereas the circumstances of Florida required only that conflict be warded off until the British evacuation was completed, the Canadian situation could not be resolved so simply. Sizeable numbers from all the Six Nations remained on British soil and when Haldiman received news in April 1783 of the peace their presence made him greatly alarmed, not relieved, to learn of the end of hostilities. What would happen to the Indians? In order to reduce their sense of betrayal Sir John Johnson, the Indian Superintendent, was sent to Niagara in July to assure those gathered there that ". . . The King still considers you his faithful Allies, as his children, and will continue to promote your happiness by his protection, and encouragement of your usual intercourse with traders with all other benefits in his power to afford you . . ."[28] Haldimand's representations to the authorities at home subsequently brought a belated recognition of the Indians' existence and a promise of sufficient assistance to confirm local assurances: in August North wrote conveying royal approval of Haldimand's steps to survey and settle lands for the Mohawks, recognizing that

> these People are justly entitled to Our peculiar Attention, and it would be far from either generous or just in Us, after our Cession of their Territories and Hunting Grounds, to forsake them. I am, therefore, authorized to acquaint you, that the King allows you to

make those Offers to them, or to any other Nations
of the friendly Indians, who may be desirous of
withdrawing themselves from the United States, and
occupying any Lands which you may allot to them
within the Province of Quebec. It is to be hoped, that
from thence they will be able to carry on their Hunting on their former Grounds, and return with their
Furs and Peltry, where the British Traders can meet
them, with their Wives and Children, in Security, and
being under our protection their Attachment to His
Majesty may continue, and this Country may enjoy
the advantage of their Trade . . .[29]

In the months following the Peace an Indian policy was
accordingly improvised, of which the cornerstone proved not so
much the sustenance of faithful friends as the diversion of potential enemies into conflict with former opponents whose goodwill
could in no way be assumed to have been won by a treaty. This
was made easier by the formulation, during 1783, of a United
States policy towards the Indians which asserted the absolute cession of all lands to the east of the Mississippi by the peace treaty, the loss of all right to territories by tribes who had fought for
the British, and which held out no more than the prospect of a
partial restoration of some Indian lands as a mark of American
generosity.[30] Against this policy, which in no way reflected the
reality of United States absence of control over Western lands
and Indians, it was comparatively simple for the British to offer
more attractive versions of Indian rights. Abandonment of Indian right to the soil was not, Johnson assured the Six Nations,
an intention of the British peacemakers:

You are not to believe or even think that by the line
which has been described it was meant to deprive you
of an extent of country of which the right of soil
belongs to, & is in yourselves as sole proprietaries as
far as the boundary line agreed upon, and established
. . . in the year 1768 at Fort Stanwix, neither can I
harbor an Idea that the United States will act so unjustly, or impolitically as to endeavor to deprive you

of any part of your Country under the pretence of
having conquered it . . .[31]

To be sure, if the notion of Indian cessions was to be maintained
as a necessary precaution, though perhaps legally superfluous
prelude, then the 1768 boundary represented the last formal
agreement between the whites and the Six Nations. If, however,
its terms were to be considered as congruous with the realities of
relations fifteen years later, then the British interpretation was as
at variance with facts as was that of the Americans. The revolutionary conflict had reduced the Iroquois lands to a devastated
condition: thirty villages, situated west of the Mohawk, had, by
the spring of 1780, included only two left undamaged by war. It
was true that the losses were by no means confined to the Indians. The settlers had suffered heavy and continuous losses in a
huge extent of some 50,000 square miles: Tryon County alone
was said, in June 1783, to number in its population 300 widows
and 2,000 orphaned children.[32] The likelihood of the Six Nations
either recovering or being restored to their ancestral lands was,
therefore, remote in the extreme. By November, 1783, however,
Haldimand had concluded that the best solution of the Indian
question would be the recognition of the land lying between the
1768 treaty boundary and the limits assigned to Canada by the
recent peace, as belonging entirely to the Indians, with British
and Americans permitted there only for trade, not for settlement.

This proposal has been seen as "the essence of the concept of
the neutral Indian barrier state," whose purpose would be the
blocking of further American settlement.[33] Even if, however, the
scheme had received the immediate and whole-hearted backing of
imperial policy, it could not have provided a satisfactory solution
to the problems of the staunchest and most vulnerable ally of the
British among the Six Nations, the Mohawk tribe. As early as
1768 the Treaty of Fort Stanwix had reduced their lands to an
extent entirely surrounded by settlement: the guarantee of the
sanctity of their remaining tract had weight only by virtue of the
special relationship maintained between them and Sir William
Johnson.[34] After a war in which Joseph Brant had been

depicted, however unjustly, as an outstanding practitioner of savage cruelties, his elder sister, Mary, being renowned for her association with Sir William and her continuing influence over the Iroquois,[35] there was less possibility of a satisfactory settlement of differences between the Mohawk and the Americans than was the case with any other tribe of the Iroquois. Not only the personality and background of Joseph Brant, but also the predicament of his tribe, made him the principal spokesman in Canada of the case of the Six Nations.

During the winter of 1783-84 the question of allocating a tract of land in Canada to the Mohawks had attracted the attention of those concerned with Indian affairs in the colony. The first choice of site was on the Bay of Quinte, on the northeastern shore of Lake Ontario, but by the spring of 1784 Brant had set aside this proposal in favour of a grant of land on the Grand River, runing into Lake Erie. The determining factor in the change was said to be the anxiety expressed by the Seneca at the distance that settlement at the Bay of Quinte would establish between the two tribes. In March 1784 Brant proposed that a tract be purchased on the Grand River "for the use of the Mohawks and such of the Six Nations as are inclined to join them in that settlement." If Loyalists should also wish to settle there, more land was available in the region. The Mohawks also urged payment of a cash indemnity of some £16,000NY for their losses during the Revolution, and provisions while the settlement was being undertaken. Brant, however, stressed that he was speaking for the Six Nations in general as well as for the Mohawks in particular. In reply, Haldimand confimed that instructions to acquire the tract had been issued, and that he would recommend that those Indians "who have been firm in their allegiance to the King thro'out the War" should be indemnified for their losses. Until he received instructions, however, he could do no more than risk advancing £1500NY, clothing and provisions.[36]

In May 1784 the Crown purchased the Grand River tract from the Mississauga Indians for the sum of £1180 7s 4d. Not all the Mohawks, however, accepted the decision to change from the Bay of Quinte, and a number insisted on settling there. Once it became clear that they represented a minority—only some twenty families moved there—Haldimand urged reunification of the main body with the remaining Iroquois. It was with this purpose in mind that he had, on 25 October 1784, announced the bestowal of land extending six miles from each bank of the Grand River upon the Mohawks "as a Safe & Comfortable Retreat for them & others of the Six Nations who have either lost their Settlements within the Territory of the American States, or wish to retire from them to the British . . . [37] That this now represented ministerial intentions was confirmed by a dispatch to Haldimand from Lord Sydney, secretary of war, who viewed the prospects of retaining Indian friendship.

> I hope the People of America will treat them with kindness, indeed *if they considered* it for a moment, their own Interest would prompt them so to do, but if they should be determined to pursue a different Conduct, you may asure those unfortunate People, that they will find an Asylum within His Majesty's Dominions should they be inclined to cross the Lakes and put themselves under our Protection . . .[38]

To this retreat over a thousand Indians moved, principally from in and around the fort at Niagara, in the course of 1785. The tract contained some 675,000 acres of land which one early visitor from Scotland considered "the finest country I have yet seen . . . The plains are very extensive, with a few trees here and there interspersed, and so thinly scattered as not to require any clearing, and hardly sufficient for the necessaries of the farmer;—the soil rich, and deep clay mold . . ."[39] A census, completed in 1785, gave a total of 1843 Indians on the Grand River, the Mohawks forming the largest group of 448, but with impressive numbers of Onondagas, Cayugas and Tuscaroras. Only the Oneidas were totally absent, but the presence of 53 Creeks and Cherokees demonstrated the extent to which the upheaval of the Revolutionary years had blurred tribal identities and confused locations.

With Southerners to be found in the north, and Iroquois in

Florida, with reports at the war's close of an attempted Confederation of all the tribes that had participated in the conflict, and with the emergence of leaders such as Brant and McGillivray, who were far from representative of traditional Indian spokesmen, the transforming impact of the Revolution upon Indian society is only too evident.[40]

At Grand River, leadership of the Indian community was secured by Joseph Brant, a position which was owing to his personal talents and British recognition rather than to any continuation of ancestral or tribal status. In some measure Brant behaved like a Loyalist, though in doing so he revealed the exceptional, not the conventional, nature of his behaviour—the Brants were the only Indians from New York to submit claims to the British government for their losses.[41] Compensation was forthcoming: Mary Brant received an annual pension of £100, and her brother continued to receive half-pay as a Captain. At the end of March 1786 payment of £1,449 14s 9d was made for their war losses.[42] If the Brants were rewarded as Loyalists, their settlement in the new land was accompanied by actions which suggested a conscious desire to develop cultural affinities with their fellow exiles. Brant, at an early age responsible for the translation into Mohawk of the Gospel of St. Mark, a freemason and correspondent of his fellow British officers, urged the early establishment on the Grand River lands of a church and a school,[43] and welcomed the arrival of white settlers in the neighbourhood. Ten years after settlement had begun a Scottish visitor was deeply impressed by the thriving condition of the village and the hospitality extended to him in the Brant household:

> Tea was on the table when we came in, served up in the handomest China plate and every other furniture in proportion. After tea was over, we were entertained with music of an elegant hand organ, on which a young Indian gentleman and Mr. Clinch played alternately. Supper was served up in the same genteel stile. Our beverage, rum, brandy, Port and Madeira wines . . . we being fatigued after our journey went timeously to rest; our beds, sheets, and English blankets, equally fine and comfortable . . .

The next evening dinner was served "in the same elegant stile":

> Two slaves attended the table, the one in scarlet, the
> other in coloured clothes, with silver buckles in their
> shoes, and their shoes, and ruffles, and every other
> part of their apparel in proportion. We drank pretty
> freely after dinner, Port and Madeira wines . . . but
> were not pressed to more than we chose. Our first
> toasts were, King, Queen, Prince of Wales, and all the
> royal family of England; and next, to the prave
> fellows who drubbed the Yankies on the 4th of last
> November [the destruction of Governor St Clair's
> expedition]; all given by the landlord in regular pro-
> gression.[4]

A domestic scene is evoked of established, unquestioned loyalism
buttressed by substantial social and economic resources. In this
aspect the union of Indian and settler in a common interest had
made much headway. But Brant's prominence did not, in the last
resort, derive from a capacity to emulate English gentlemen,
even though his Canadian residence sought to copy the structure
of Johnson Hall, but from his influence upon the course of Indian affairs as they affected Anglo-American relations in the
post-war years. The division of the Iroquois, a product of war,
had become confirmed by later events. An early indication of the
impossibility of retaining or renewing the Confederacy was to be
found in the events leading up to the concluding of the Treaty of
Fort Stanwix in October 1784. In previous months conflicting interests representing the United States and the state of New York
had separately moved towards negotiations with the Indians:
both required new boundaries and more lands but disagreement
was wide on the question of constitutional powers and territorial
extent. Brant was anxious to secure a general settlement, involving tribes other than the Six Nations and also the Confederation,
and proposed that the negotiations be held at Fort Stanwix.[45] If
Brant had supposed, however, that the broadening of the
negotiations would benefit the Six Nations or his own reputation, he could not have been more mistaken: the discussions with
the New York commissioners achieved nothing and the negotia-

tions with the United States, a month later, involved only dictated terms. The Iroquois were informed that they had not become a free and independent nation by having been excluded from the peace terms "It is not so. You are a subdued people; you have been overcome in war which you entered into with us, not only, without provocation, but in violation of most sacred obligations." Brant had by that time left the meeting, while those who remained signed a brief treaty abandoning all claims to lands in Pennsylvania and the Ohio Valley, obtaining only an article which assured the Oneida and Tuscaroras possession of the lands on which they were settled.[46] That was a guarantee which proved before long absolutely worthless. For the Oneidas the process of spoliation was to begin in the following summer, when New York acquired half a million acres from them on the Unadilla, a loss temporarily assuaged by the Onandaga decision to recognize their nation as the head of the Confederacy in place of the now departed Mohawks.[47] By such steps a situation evolved, and became steadily more evident, in whch American and Canadian Iroquois developed competing and distinct organizations. After 1802 the Onondaga council fire existed together with a rival body at Grand River.[48] The peace, as much as the war, had divided the Six Nations.

For two decades Brant continued intermittently to play off British against American efforts to secure an Indian alliance. If his residence within British territory seemed to render impracticable his aim of preserving an independence from both nations, a continuous conflict with the Canadian authorities over the terms on which the Grand River grant was held, stimulated a need to maintain a distance and assert his status. The dispute turned upon the right of Brant to dispose of land from the Grand River tract. The official view was that this contravened the terms of the Proclamation of 7 October 1763, a document which still "has the force of a statute in Canada and has never been repealed."[49] The particular reference was to the prohibition of land purchases from the Indians and the injunction

that no private person do presume to make any Purchase from the said Indians of any Lands reserved to the

said Indians, within those parts of our Colonies where,
We have thought proper to allow Settlement; but that, if
at any Time any of the said Indians should be inclined to
dispose of the said Lands, the same shall be purchased
only for Us, in our Name, at some public Meeting or
Assembly of the said Indians, to be held for that Purpose by the Governor or Commander in Chief of our
Colony respectively within which they shall lie . . .[50]

Brant had treated the grant as land which could be sold or leased to
others, a practice which was to lead to a lengthy process of official
opposition. He claimed that acceptance of the grant had assumed
that the land would be their own. The decision had been made at a
time when

we still had opportunities after the war of providing for
ourselves in the free and independent manner natural to
Indians; unhappily for us we have been made ac-
quainted too late with the first real intention of
Ministry, that is that they never intended us to have it in
our power to alienate any part of the lands, and here we
have even been prohibited from taking tenants on them,
it having been represented as inconsistent for us being
but King's allies to have king's subjects as tenants; consequently I suppose their real meaning was, we should in
a manner be but tenants ourselves, as for me I see no
difference in it, any farther than that we are as yet not
free,—they seemingly intended to forbid us any other
use of the lands than that of sitting down or walking on
them. It plainly appears by this that their motives can be
no other than to tie us down in such manner, as to have
us entirely at their disposal for what services they may in
future want from us, and in case we should be warned
out & obliged to remove, the lands would then fall to
them with our improvements & labour . . .[51]

The land had been sold to Loyalists and Brant poiinted out that the
Indians had received no compensation for the hunting-grounds and
woodlands lost as a consequence of their adherence to the Crown.[52]
Although a compromise was reached in 1798, by which the land

already transferred to individuals was surrendered to the Crown by the Six Nations and placed under trusteeship, the Indian tract continued steadily to diminish in extent until, after 1840, only 55,000 acres remained in the hands of the Six Nations. At mid-century the total Indian population stood at only 2,500, of whom 800 Mohawks constituted the largest group. Although the grand council was still held at Grand River, the significance and strength of the Indian community had greatly diminished.[53]

A recent study of the Iroquois in the Revolution concludes a comparison of the lots of the nations in Canada and the United States by the judgment that "if we were to evaluate which fared better in their respective situations, we should probably have to name the Grand River Iroquois."[54] True though this might have been in material terms, it proved to be the case that the status of these Indians in Canada remained legally and constitutionally controversial for well over a century and a half following their removal from their ancestral territory. In contrast with the United States, no treaties of any kind were concluded between the British authorities and the Iroquois after 1783. Relations were not without their moments of tension and causes of friction—Brant dabbled in speculation and perhaps worse during his acquaintance with Aaron Burr—but the Six Nations remained in general well-disposed towards the Crown. In the wake of the 1837 rebellion in Upper Canada William Johnson Kerr, grandson of Molly Brant, wrote in furious denunciation of Joseph Hume, the persistent British parliamentary radical, who had insinuated that the Six Nations had again taken to the warpath. They had, Kerr asserted, merely "turned out with alacrity, and joined their brethren the Militia in defence of the Country, its laws and institutions." It was not they but "Mr Humes intimate and confidential friends and correspondents who were"rising in the Country, with Knife in one hand a firebrand in the other." For nearly two centuries, Kerr concluded, the friendship of the Six Nations for Great Brtitain had endured. "And to their honor be it spoken, they have neither Indian Radicals nor Indian Rebels amongst them."[55] Although in due course a message from the Colonial Secretary offered assurances that neither the Queen nor her people doubted for a moment the loyal attachment of the Indians, their status remained obstinately obscure. Efforts to secure recognition as allies, not subjects—no final preference had ever been indicated by the authorities—were launched but without success: in 1839, in 1890, and again in 1920 the claim was denied.[56] The gain to the Indians, if successful, would have been freedom from interference with their institutions on tribal lands, a right claimed by the Government of Canada, after 1867, by virtue of Section 91 (24) of the British North America Act.[57] Attempts to secure international recognition were made, without success: in 1923 a petition was taken to the League of Nations by a Grand River chief travelling on a Six Nations Confederacy Council passport. Despite this, the Chief reached Geneva but there failed to secure a hearing of the case before the League.[58] Some thirty years later a further attempt to secure international acknowledgement was made when a case was created on the basis of Article III of the Jay treaty. This had acknowledged the existence of the Indians when providing for the free passage of individuals and favorable terms for the passage of goods between the United States and British North America. An exemption was declared by which "the Indians passing or repassing with their own proper Goods and effects of whatever nature [shall not] pay for the same any Impost or Duty whatever. But Goods in Bales or other large Packages unusual among Indians shall not be considered as Goods belonging bona fide to Indians."[59] In 1956 a Six Nations Indian from a Quebec reserve carried to the Supreme Court of Canada a claim which invoked this clause of the Treaty as cause for the return of duties on goods brought from the United States. His case was dismissed on the grounds that legislation had never been enacted to sanction or implement the Treaty. One cannot help regretting that this was why the claim was rejected since the items involved hardly appeared to represent traditional artifacts: doubtless the problem of defining a "large package" provided a reason for declining to assess the articles in question against the clause of the treaty—they comprised an oil heater, a refrigerator, and a washing machine. It was concluded that, without specific legislation to call upon, Indians were as subject as Canadian citizens in general to the laws of the country.[60] Three years later the issue of the distinctiveness or normality of the Indians' legal status was considered in the case of *Logan v. Attorney-General of*

Canada. A series of disturbances and disagreements had occurred as a result of attempts by some Indians on the Grand River reserve to remove the elected council and restore government by hereditary chiefs. In March 1959 minor disorders were suppressed by the Royal Canadian Mounted Police and in September Mr. Justice King dismissed an action which sought to confirm Indian independence within the reserve. His opinion clearly asserted his view of the long-debated question:

> those of the Six Nations Indians so settling on such lands, together with their posterity, by accepting the protection of the Crown then owed allegiance to the Crown and thus, became subjects of the Crown. Thus, the said Six Nations Indians from having been the faithful allies of the Crown became, instead, loyal subjects of the Crown . . .[61]

If an historian may be sufficiently impertinent to convey approval of a legal judgement, it would seem that this opinion, though describing events in far too absolute a form—the Six Nations had been no more than intermittently faithful before 1784, and were not conspicuously loyal on all occasions after that date— was essentially correct. With the settlement of the Iroquois on the Grand River a refuge was provided for the dispossessed. The Six Nations had no grounds on which to claim that a bond existed between themselves and the tract granted them, such as marked traditional Indian links to the soil. Henceforth they would be subjects, and no less or more loyal than their white neighbors. Nevertheless, any community compelled to wait 175 years for official acceptance of its loyalty has reason to consider itself to be viewed with unreasonable suspicion. The first Americans received the dubious distinction of being very belatedly recognized as the last Loyalists.

THE REVEREND JOHN STUART
MOHAWK MISSIONARY
AND RELUCTANT LOYALIST

BY

G. A. RAWLYK

═══════════════════

THE Reverend John Stuart was not only an extremely conscientious and gifted Anglican missionary to the Mohawks in pre-Revolutionary New York. He was also the founder of the Church of England in Upper Canada as well as the "spiritual father"[1] to the Reverend John Strachan. Stuart and his Kingston friend, Richard Cartwright, had, in the first decade of the 19th century, a profound impact on Strachan's evolving political and social ideas. And they may, therefore, be regarded as critically important links in the ideological chain which connects the articulated Loyalist thought of the 1770s with the Upper Canadian Tory conceptual framework of the post-War of 1812 period.

His friends affectionately called him the "little Gentleman."[2] Stuart was a huge man—well over six feet. John Beverly Robinson, the distinguished Upper Canadian politician and Chief Justice, remembered Stuart as being

> not corpulent, and not thin—but with fine masculine features, expanded chest, erect figure; straight, well-formed limbs, and a free, manly carriage, improved by a fondness in his youth for athletic exercises, particularly fencing.

As far as Robinson was concerned, he had "seen no one who came so fully up to the idea one is led to form of a fine old Roman—a man capable of enduring and defying anything in a good cause; incapable—absolutely incapable of stooping to anything in the least degree mean or unworthy."[3]

The Reverend J.H.B. Mountain (the son of the first Bishop of Quebec) remembered Stuart as a "man of a higher stamp than the rest." Stuart had "a powerful frame . . . of a somewhat stately bearing as conceiving himself the lineal descendant of the legitimate Monarch, but merging that pride in the humility of his ministerial function."[4] Strachan, found him to be "a truly amiable man." But he was more than this:

> His manners were gentle and conciliatory, and his character such as led him rather to win men by kindness and persuasion, than to awe and alarm them by the terrors of authority. His sermons, composed in plain and nervous language, were recommended by the affectionate manner of his delivery, and not unfrequently found a way to the consciences of those who had long been insensible to any real religious convictions.[5]

Stuart, for Strachan and others, was also a man with amazing physical energy. In his pastoral ministry he was "assiduous, diligent and attentive." And his piety, Strachan observed, "was deep-felt, rational, fervent but unostentatious."[6] According to Robinson, as well, Stuart possessed a "natural simplicity of character and contempt of ostentation." He was, all seemed to agree, "loved and respected by everyone." "No Clergyman,"Robinson observed

> could be more universally respected and beloved than he was by his people. . . . He could not recede from what he thought to be right, under the pressure of *any* circumstance; but he abhorred contention, and there was, indeed, too much natural dignity of character about him to permit him to involve himself in anything of the kind.[7]

John Stuart was born on March 10, 1740, near Harris' Ferry, Paxton Township, Pennsylvania.[8] His father, Andrew, it is claimed, was the grandson of the Duke of Monmouth, the ill-fated son of Charles II. Andrew Stuart had emigrated to Pennsylvania in 1730 from County Tyrone, Ireland. He came to the New World as a strict Presbyterian eagerly searching for religious freedom and commercial prosperity. Stuart married Mary Dinwiddie, the sister of Robert Dinwiddie, Lieutenant-Governor of Virginia. John was their first child. He had three brothers but only two of them reached adulthood and both of them—as Strachan put it—"having been in the worst of times, staunch supporters of the cause of American liberty." At an early age John Stuart "evinced a disposition for serious studies." As a youth he received "a good classical education" and retained until his death in 1811 "a relish for the beauties of Greek and Latin authors." This interest in the Classics was further developed at the College of Philadelphia where Stuart was greatly influenced by the president of the college, the Reverend William Smith. Smith had been ordained in 1753 as a minister in the Scottish Episcopal Church and he played a critically important role in persuading Stuart to abandon his Presbyterianism for Anglicanism.

When Stuart graduated from the College of Philadelphia in 1763 he not only possessed a B.A. and a sophisticated grasp of Greek and Latin but also a desire to be ordained into the Anglican ministry. But Stuart's father had other ideas. In 1763 Andrew Stuart was vociferously opposed to Anglicanism and did everything in his power to prevent his son from being ordained. John reluctantly abandoned his plan "out of deference to his father" and instead became a schoolmaster.

After seven years of teaching, John finally persuaded his father, in 1770, to permit him "to follow his own inclination." According to Strachan, Andrew Stuart had been "struck with the greatness" of his son's sacrifice and "the unequivocal proof of the excellence of his character." Obviously, the older Stuart's resistance had been slowly broken down by an unusually persistent son. In the process John Stuart had proven the validity of his belief in a paternalistic and deferential society. He had shown that with patience, love and affection, reason and order would eventually prevail.

In the summer of 1770 Stuart was ordained in London. But before undertaking his voyage to England, Stuart had come to the attention of Sir William Johnson, Superintendent of Indian Affairs and a very active member of the Society of the Propagation of the Gospel. As might be expected, the Reverend William Smith had made Johnson aware of his protégé in March 1770. Smith knew that Johnson desperately wanted Anglican missionaries to minister to the Six Nations of the Iroquois in general and to his Mohawk neighbors in particular. Smith recommended Stuart as a person

> who, I think, I can answer for, on long Experience as an excellent Scholar, [with] a fine Temper, & I am persuaded you will be happy in Him, & he in you, if a tolerable Settlement can be got for him, under your Protection.[9]

In reply, the delighted Johnson observed:

> I am glad to find you all so sensible of the Necessity there is for using all possible endeavours to promote a Cause which through many unfortunate Circumstance has hitherto met with little futherance. I need not enlarge on the many weighty reasons there are for continuing that Spirit, and those endeavours, as it must be obvious that without the utmost zeal and attention to these matters, all our laudable Wishes must . . . be rendered abortive.[10]

What was worrying Johnson and other concerned Anglicans in New York in 1770 was the fragile loyalty of the Iroquois to the British Crown. The Stamp Act crisis had shown, among other things, how vulnerable the Imperial authorities were to Patriot intimidation. Iroquois support for the Imperial cause had to be cultivated. The Reverend Charles Inglis, of Trinity Church, New York, cut to the heart of the problem when he declared:

> The Savages on this Continent are a numerous, fierce and warlike people. It is of the utmost Consequence to the Colonies to secure their Friendship & attach them to

our Interest. Reason and Experience demonstrate this cannot be so effectually done as by proselytizing them to Christianity, as professed by the Church of England.[11]

For Inglis and Johnson, S.P.G. missionaries would make the Iroquois "serviceable to the State" and supporters of the British cause in North America.[12] Evangelical missionaries from New England, on the other hand, would transform the Indians into Patriot firebrands. The American Revolution would prove the validity of the Inglis-Johnson hypothesis.

Stuart seemed almost too good to be true. For years the Iroquois had to be satisfied with the dregs of the Anglican missionary effort, much to the disgust of Johnson. But, in 1770, at last there was a man with physical presence, and considerable natural ability who had "a particular Desire to enter upon an *Indian Mission*."[13] After his ordination in London, it was reported to Johnson that Stuart had "departed full of Joy at the Prospect of being placed under your direction."[14]

Stuart returned to New York in November, 1770, and quickly made his way to Fort Hunter, his Mohawk mission located just a few miles from Johnson's residence on the Mohawk River. Almost immediately, under Johnson's guidance, Stuart began to try to learn the Mohawk language "as it is so Essential to his Success."[15] He obviously was delighted with his general situation. From the beginning he was "much Esteemed"[16] by the Mohawks and he was also very much liked by the Dutch inhabitants of the region who flocked to hear him preach. Stuart, who considered himself a refined eighteenth century gentleman, found at Fort Hunter not only a Church and a Parsonage but also a fertile cleared farm. The Chapel had been built years before and contained, among other things, "a beautiful gift of Communion Plate which had been presented by Queen Anne and on which was inscribed the Royal Cypher and coat-of-arms."[17]

Each Sunday Stuart had two services at Fort Hunter—the first was in Mohawk. He was able to read "Divine Service . . . in their own Language"[18] but he could not preach sermons without the help of an interpreter. The second service was in

English and was aimed at the non-Mohawk residents of the region. Stuart also sometimes itinerated during the week conducting services at Mohawk settlements such as Canajoharie. He also conducted a school at Fort Hunter. His obvious enthusiasm and commitment impressed Johnson and Inglis. As far as Inglis was concerned Stuart was "a worthy Man, the Indians are fond of him, & in a good Disposition to receive the Truths of Christianity."[19] After his first full year at Fort Hunter, Stuart perceived two major problems. First, too many of the Mohawk residents were "much addicted to Drunkenes" and second, he could not preach to them in their own language. To deal with the first problem, he encouraged the sachems to attempt "to suppress a custom so injurious to their temporal as well as spiritual welfare."[20] To deal with the second, in March of 1772, he "thought it expedient to procure a young Man of their own Nation (who understands English) to reside with me as a private Tutor & public Interpreter." "By his assistance," Stuart reported to the S.P.G. on July 20, 1772, "I have given them a Sermon every Sunday since March."[21] The young man selected by Stuart to master "the barren and difficult Mohawk language was Joseph Brant. Brant, in 1772, was twenty-nine years old and a protégé of Sir William Johnson who had him educated at the Reverend Eleazar Wheelock's famous school located at Lebanon, Connecticut. Until Brant's death in Upper Canada in November 1807, he and Stuart would be close friends and their two careers would be strangely intertwined.

Brant's arrival spurred Stuart to even greater missionary efforts. Stuart needed all the considerable energy at his disposal to deal with the growing demand on his services. The Mohawks at Canajoharie were demanding more and more attention from Stuart. And since Johnstown was without a minister after 1773, Stuart "frequently officiated there."[22] Apparently Stuart thrived on what Johnson would call his "assiduous" labour. In the summer of 1772, for example, Stuart could report to the S.P.G.

> Upon the whole I have the Pleasure to acquaint the Society that my Ministry in this Place (through God's Blessing) appears to have been successful—a more af-

fecting Sense of Religion—a more constant Attend-
ance on public Worship, and a visible Amendment in
the Lives of many, are the happy Fruits which daily
appear. . . .
N.B. The Number of Commts on Whitsunday last
     was Indian 14
          White 13.[23]

Despite the fact that he could not as yet master the Mohawk
language, under the guidance of Brant, Stuart by early 1774 had
learned to "read to them in their own language . . . the Liturgy,
with Administration, of the Sacraments of Baptism & the Lord's
Supper, Marriage & the Office for the Burial of the Dead." But
of greater importance he could "converse tolerably well with
them on common subjects."[24] With the help of Brant and
Paulus, another educated Mohawk, Stuart was preparing in 1773
and 1774 a Mohawk translation of "the Gospel of St. Mark—
with a large & plain Exposition of the Church Catechism & a
compendious History of the Bible." Sir William Johnson had encouraged the translation project and had also promised to
finance its eventual publication. But a few weeks before the
manuscript was "ready for the Press," Johnson died.[25] His
death on July 9, 1774, radically altered the political and strategic
situation in Northern New York and may be seen as a critical
turning point in the Anglo-American battle for what George
Washington would call the "Rising American Empire."

William Johnson's nephew and son-in-law, Guy Johnson, suc-
ceeded the former as Superintendant of Indian Affairs while
William's son, John, received his father's military commission as
Major-General of the Militia. Neither man came close to filling
William Johnson's shoes and this considerably weakened the
British position in the northern frontier region of New York.
William Johnson's death had occurred when Iroquois-white ten-
sions over land ownership were precipitating violence and blood-
shed. One month following Johnson's death, the somewhat dis-
oriented Stuart observed:

Affairs in America are, at present, in a very critical
Situation & particularly in Regard to the Indians—the
Indians to the Southward are actually in Arms, having
murdered several Hundreds of white People,—the *five
Nations* here profess themselves Friends to the English
yet, But are thought (by good Judges) to be wavering in
their Judgment—and should the War become general,
my Situation wou'd be by no means an eligible one.[26]

Stuart was concerned in 1774 about his "eligible Situation" in
more than one respect. Soon after the death of his father in 1774
(his mother had passed away two years earlier), Stuart became
engaged to Jane Okill the twenty-seven-year-old daughter of the
Chruch-warden of Philadelphia's Christ Church. They were married in Philadelphia on October 12, 1775. They eventually had eight
children; five sons and three daughters. Strachan described Stuart
the father in the following manner:

he was kind without being improperly indulgent; he
knew beyond most men how to temper firmness with
kindness, and parental authority with winning attention. His love for his children was frequently manifested
at the expense of his personal ease and comfort; he
derived more pleasure from conferring benefits on them
than from indulging his most favourable and innocent
inclinations.

Then Strachan went to what he considered to be at the heart of
Strachan's social attitudes and his preoccupation with establishing
and perpetuating his dynasty in the New World:

He spared no expense in giving them a good education,
and in qualifying them to appear with advantage in the
world. He proceeded upon the grand principle that by
inspiring his children with the noblest virtues and
cultivating their minds he would unite them more
closely together, and leave a purer protection to the
younger branches of his family than silver and gold. The
elder would be able and eager from principle to assist
the younger, and be in the place of a father.[27]

The "grand principle" so eloquently described by Strachan was the cement which eventually gave form and substance to Stuart's conservative political ideology.

All of Stuart's contemporaries agreed that he had what was called a "remarkable . . . knowledge of the human character."[28] He hated controversy and did everything in his power to steer clear of polarizing situations. In addition, throughout his adult life, he accepted, without question, a belief in a stratified, organic and ordered society. To those who had been placed above him, he willingly offered his obedience and his respect. But by those who had been placed beneath him in the social order, he expected to be treated in precisely the same way he treated his superiors. Stuart's views concerning society made him especially happy to be an Anglican and, moreover, gave him a special sense of fulfillment in being a S.P.G. missionary to the Mohawks. He was particularly proud of the fact that he had been "the Instrument of spreading the Knowledge of His Gospel among the Heathen.[29] He had a deep psychological need to be regarded by the Mohawks "as a father among his children."[30]

News about the outbreak of hostilities at Lexington in April 1775 introduced even more confusion to an already confused and disoriented Iroquois population. In May, Guy Johnson ordered all Yankee missionaries to leave the land of the Iroquois. They were to stay away "until the difficulties between Great Britain and the Colonies are settled—as it cannot be supposed but the N. England missionaries, from their Native attachment to their country, may be led some way or other to bias the Indians against government."[31] In response to Johnson's anti-Patriot policy, the Tryon County Committee of Safety immediately attempted to impose its authority over the Fort Hunter region. Realizing the special role that Stuart played among the Mohawks, the Committee decided that it would be both "Imprudent as well as Impolitic" to compel him to leave Fort Hunter. The Committee members did not want to alienate the Mohawks but they wanted to intimidate Stuart. Apparently Stuart was instructed "not to meddle in the quarrel between the colonies and England and not to give aid or comfort to the enemies of America, under pain of being subject to the full penalty of the law."[32]

The summer months of 1775 in Northern New York witnessed a furious battle between Johnson and the Patriots for the support of the Iroquois. In August, the Continental Congress sent Commissioners to the Iroquois in order to win their support or else their neutrality. A military expedition was being planned against Quebec and the Congress was eager to protect the vulnerable American rear. During the conference held in Albany, the Commissioners were urged not to remove Stuart from Fort Hunter:

> our father the minister . . . resides among the Mohawks, and was sent them by the King. He does not meddle in civil affairs, but instructs them in the way to heaven. He absolutely refuses to attend to any political matters, and says they do not belong to him. They beg he may continue in peace among them. . . . It would occasion great disturbance, was he to be taken away. The King sent him to them, and they would look upon it as taking away one of their own body.

On the following day, 1 September 1775 the Commissioners replied that they agreed with the Iroquois description of Stuart as a missionary "who did not concern himself with the affairs of this world, but was earnestly engaged in conducting you to happiness, and instructing you in the reverence due the great God who governs the universe." "Brothers," declared the Commissioners, "such a man we love, and we are desirous of his remaining quiet and happy with you."[33] While the fate of Stuart was thus being debated, the Mohawk missionary was preparing for his wedding in Philadelphia.

On his journey back to Fort Hunter in October, 1775, Stuart made his S.P.G. superiors aware of his delicate and vulnerable position. His protector, Guy Johnson, had left New York for Quebec taking with him a number of Iroquois and European Loyalists. The Mohawks, Stuart reported, "are much attached to me, and have publickly declared that they will support & defend me, while I reside among them. "And I am sorry to say," he went on, "that I depend (at present) more on their Protection than that of those from whom more might be expected."[34]

Despite the turmoil around him, Stuart continued to minister to his Mohawk congregation. His wife provided him with support and much needed companionship. And the birth of their first child, a son, on 29 June 1776 brought them both great joy and contentment. In June 1776 Stuart was thirty-six years old. He had been very fortunate in marrying a wealthy woman who possessed both money and land. This good fortune helped to drive away some of his worries about the future and about his declining social prestige. But the Patriot-Johnson battle for the minds and the military support of the Iroquois disturbed him. In the summer of 1776 when the Declaration of Independence was being formulated and endorsed Stuart really did not understand what the political turmoil was all about. He was obsessed with his marriage and his missionary work. And he was obviously puzzled by the events and the rhetoric moving the Thirteen Colonies from "Resistance to Revolution."

Because of his close association with the Johnson family, Stuart was carefully watched throughout the latter part of 1776 and the early months of 1777 by the Tryon County Committee of Safety. Despite this, he "constantly performed divine service without omitting the prayers for the king, as prescribed in the liturgy."[35] Then, in the spring of 1777, General Nicholas Herkimer, the president of the Committee of Safety discovered what some people considered to be some incriminating Stuart letters. But upon closer examination the letters were found to be harmless.[36] Nevertheless, he felt under greater pressure and expected at any moment to be driven from Fort Hunter by the Patriots. Their opportunity came soon after a number of his Mohawk parishioners decided to join General Burgoyne's invading army. When news of "Gentleman Johnny's" defeat reached Tryon County in late October 1777 the Committee of Safety urged its supporters to eradicate the Anglican presence from their midst. An armed mob attacked Stuart's house, plundered his property and looted the Church. And the Anglican minister, after being incarcerated for four days, was "confined to Parole, and confined to the Limits of the Town of Schenectady."[37] Stuart later learned that his Church had been "imployed as a Tavern, the Barrel of Rum placed in the Reading Desk" and then it was "used as a Stable."[38]

A disheartened and bewildered Stuart made his way to Schenectady. With him were his wife, his infant son and his Black slaves. Stuart found himself in most disagreeable circumstances. He could not draw on his salary in London, he lacked proper clothing and his wife was soon pregnant again. Then on 11 July 1778 the Albany Committee for Detecting Conspiracies declared that he was "a declared Enemy to the Liberties of America" and consequently ordered "him down the Country." Two weeks later Stuart was instructed to "repair with his family forthwith to the State of Connecticut until his exchange could be procured, and that he sett off in four Days after this Resolution is delivered to him, and on his failure to comply herewith it is ordered that he be put into close confinement."[39]

On June 27 Stuart appeared before the Albany Committee. He did everything in his power "to convince them that he had not corresponded with the enemy, and that he was ready and willing to enter into any agreement for the faithful performance of such matters as might be enjoyned him." The Committee, on hearing his defence, resolved that Stuart

> enter into Parole not to do or say any Thing in opposition to the Measures pursued by the Congress of the United States of America, or by the Legislative or executive Powers of either of the said States, and that he shall and will not hold any correspondence by word or Deed upon Politikal Matters with any of the enemies of the said United States of America . . . and not to depart the Limits of the Town of Schenectady without permission from one of the Members of this Board.[40]

After agreeing to this arrangement, Stuart returned to his Schenectady residence. A year later he wrote to his close Philadelphia friend, the Reverend William White, then Chaplain to the Continental Congress, about his general situation. He hoped to be permitted to return to Fort Hunter once "the military operations are suspended in this quarter." He found Schenectady "rather disagreeable, being deserted by almost all my congregation" apart from "three Families." He had, moreover, "not preached within these two years past." Stuart asked White to look after his wife's Pennsylvania property "either money or anything else, well secured by bonds or mortgages."[41] What Stuart intended to do in 1778 was to wait until the war was over and then put all the pieces back together in New York and Pennsylvania. He had no desire to follow some of his S.P.G. associates and apply "for liberty to remove to Canada."[42]

But, much to Stuart's disgust, peace, order and stability did not soon return to the Mohawk River Valley. In late October, 1778, Walter Butler and Joseph Brant played key roles in the infamous "Cherry Valley Massacre." Then, in the summer of 1779 the Americans counterattacked as General John Sullivan and General James Clinton drove their armies into the heart of the Iroquois Country. Because of the expected bloody warfare in the Schenectady area, Stuart moved to Albany for a brief time but on June 23 he was ordered to return to his home.[43]

In the spring of 1780, the pro-British Iroquois returned to the Mohawk Valley "infuriated rather than humbled by the punishment which Gen. Sullivan inflicted on them in the course of the preceding summer."[44] Once again the Stuarts, in June, felt compelled to "take sanctuary in Albany." The move was accomplished with only minutes to spare and Stuart "could see several houses in flames from our windows." It is interesting to note that Stuart referred to the pro-British Iroquois invaders as the "enemy."[45]

During his second Albany sojourn, Stuart experienced, as Strachan put it, "much civility from Genl. Schuyler and obtained permission to visit Philadelphia."[46] For months he had been trying to persuade the authorities to permit him to deal with various pressing family problems in Philadelphia. While in Philadelphia, he made the necessary arrangements to protect his wife's property and he also renewed many old friendships. In addition, he almost found himself tarred and feathered by a furious Philadelphia mob. According to Stuart's son,

> happening to pass whilst in that city through one of its thoroughfares, his progress was arrested by a crowd which a young man was haranguing, at the moment, on the course of public events. Hearing a remark from a bystander flattering to the personal appearance of the orator, Mr. Stuart unguardedly made a caustic though

humorous remark on the same subject, and then proceeded to his Lodgings. The observation circulating
through the crowd, aroused considerable indignation
and the meeting adjourned for the purpose of inflicting
personal chastisement on the person who had been so
bold as to utter it. Mr. Stuart received timely notice
from a friend of these hostile intentions, but nothing
could prevail on him to retreat before the impending
danger. He resolved to face it, not fly from it. For-
tunately, the Rev. Mr. White and others interfered, and
the indignation of the people was appeased.[47]

It is not surprising that the Philadelphia sojourn had a considerable impact on Stuart's thinking. The city he had returned to
in 1780 was radically different from the Philadelphia he had known
before the Revolution. Instead of deferential order there was the
rule of the mob. Instead of commercial men of honour there were
what Stuart spitefully called the "private Robbers."[48] Instead of
the warmth of a closely knit family there was the bitterness of
ideological conflict. What Stuart had slowly come to realize in
Philadelphia was that the Revolutionary madness had transformed
what had been Anglo-American civilization into republican an-
archy.

On his return to Schenectady, later in 1780, Stuart resolved to
move to Quebec. "Considering the present situation of Affairs in
this Part of the Province," he wrote to White on November 13, "I
am fully persuaded that I cannot possibly live here secure, either in
regard to ourselves or Property during the ensuing Season." "This
Place is likely to be a Frontier," he pointed out "and will probably
be burnt if the Enemy can effect it." Stuart had heard about
staunch New York Loyalists being butchered by the Anglo- Iroquois invaders and he did not want to see what might happen to
someone who had carefully walked the knife-edge of neutrality
since the beginning of hostilities. But there were two other reasons
explicitly mentioned by Stuart in his letter to White. First, Stuart
had reacted violently and with disgust to the way in which he had
"lost a considerable Part of my stocks while in Philadelphia." He
was convinced that he had been swindled by unprincipled en-
trepreneurs and he never wanted to see them or their associates

again. The second reason was that Mrs. Stuart had given her
"Approbation & Consent" to the proposed move. Despite the fact
that she had three tiny children and despite the fact that she was
strongly attached to her Philadelphia family, she agreed "to
emigrate to Canada."[49]

By November 1780 Stuart had made "Application for an Exchange." But for a variety of reasons his request was not successful
until the spring of the following year. There is some evidence to
suggest that Governor Haldimand delayed the exchange thinking
that Stuart might yet provide the British with useful intelligence.
The Americans, on the other hand, apparently wanted in exchange
for Stuart more than the British at first were prepared to give.

In April 1781 Stuart informed White that the move to Quebec
was to take place almost immediately. Once again he attempted to
articulate some of the reasons for the move. He knew that White
would realize that the decision was a momentous one and one that
Stuart had found great difficulty making. For Stuart had to admit
that one of his principal vices had always been procrastination.
"The truth is" he once confessed, "I postpone and procrastinate
till negligence becomes in me, inexcusable."[50] "Believe me, Dear
Sir," Stuart implored White,

> I have had Occasion to exert all my Resolution before I
> cou'd venture on the Difficulties that present themselves
> as the probable Concomitants of this Journey; but from
> a Variety of Circumstances peculiar to my personal and
> local Situation, I had no Alternative; Therefore, let the
> Event be as it will, I shall not think myself accountable
> for Consequences—the more especially as Mrs. Stuart is
> perfectly reconciled to the Expediency and the Necessity
> of the Measure.

Stuart was resigned to make the best of his fate in the Canadian
wilderness. He had therefore resolved

> to leave nothing behind me here that may impose any
> necessity upon me of returning to this Place (provided
> such a Thing possible) when the War is at an End—I can
> Dispose of all my Effects either for Cash or good Bills

on Canada, my Negroes being personal Property, I take
with me—one of which being a young Man Capable of
bearing Arms, I have given £100 Security to send back a
white Prisoner in his Stead.[51]

Two days before he and his family left Schenectady for Quebec
Stuart scribbled his final American letter to White. Perhaps he was
making a terrible mistake after all. The move was, according to
Stuart, "a measure fraught with danger & difficulty, and eligible in
no other view than as the lesser evil." His wife, he had to admit,
"submits to it rather from Necessity than Choice, and I cannot but
lament the necessity that puts her Affection to so severe a trial." If
Stuart was a reluctant Loyalist, his wife was even more reluctant.
Consequently, Stuart could only "hope she will never have reason
to repent of it."[52]

On October 6, 1781 the Stuart family finally touched Quebec
soil. Eventually they would settle permanently at Kingston on Lake
Ontario where Stuart would play a key role in helping to shape the
contours of Upper Canadian development. During his early years
in Kingston he was never absolutely certain that he had made a wise
decision in becoming a Loyalist. He was tempted, despite
everything, to return to the United States. In November 1785 for
example, he informed White, now a Bishop of the American
Episcopal Church, that

Notwithstanding all my Philosophy & Christian Resignation to my Fate, I must confess that even writing to
a Friend in that Quarter of the world, recals Ideas to my
mind not the most pleasing. But I must banish them, &
make virtue of necessity. Perhaps I could not live so
happy, even in Philada, as at Cataraque [Kingston]—
I'll endeavour to persuade myself of it.[53]

But by 1788 Stuart had grown—as he put it—"quite contented and
resigned to my Fate."[54]   A decade later, he had absolutely no
doubts. He maintained to White

how mysterious are the Ways of Providence. How short
sighted are We. Some Years ago I thought it a great

hardship to be banished into this Wilderness and wou'd
have imagined myself completely happy cou'd I have ex-
changed it for a Place in the delightful City of Philadelphia. Now the best Wish we can form for our dearest
Friends is to have them remove to us.[55]

For Stuart, the United States represented "Taxes, Poverty &
Tyranny."[56] On the other hand, Upper Canada was a manifesta-
tion of British "Peace, Order and Good Government." Stuart
might have added, as an aside, "Property." For, by 7 January
1798, he could boast that "we have now in the Family more than
7,000 Acres, and I hope to make it ten, before the present year ex-
pires."[57]

Stuart died on 15 August 1811 "after a short but painful illness,
which he supported with Christian fortitude and resignation."[58] All
Kingston mourned the loss of the distinguished "little Gentleman."
The reluctant and procrastinating Loyalist had become a founder
of the Church he loved in a British Colony he had helped to mould
according to his own peculiar conservative world-view. It was a
view which stressed the crucial importance of the mutuality of
obligation and responsibility in creating a proper concept of community.

THE LOYALISTS
IN THE WEST INDIES, 1783-1834

BY

WALLACE BROWN

=========

THIS paper concerns the exodus of the American Loyalists to southern waters and their experiences in their new homes.

Let me start with a definition or two. Since there is no word encompassing Bermuda, the Bahamas and the West Indies, I shall use the term "the islands." And because this paper deals almost entirely with the Bahamas, Jamaica and Dominica, a restriction to those areas is usually called for today. As in the case of Quebec and Nova Scotia, a persuasive case can be made for designating as Loyalists the islanders who failed to join the American rebellion, but I shall apply Loyalist, Tory, refugee and emigre only to the loyal denizens of "the old thirteen" colonies and occasionally to those of East and West Florida. The old inhabitants of the Bahamas were desparagingly called "Conchs" by the Loyalists after that delicious, still popular, shellfish. As late as 1824 the name still caused resentment, but I shall use it neutrally throughout.

The story of the Loyalists in the islands is sufficiently ill-known to warrant the recital of some of the elementary facts that I and others have discussed. Their arrival must be placed in the context of the entire Loyalist diaspora. As one island refugee put it: "the War never occasioned half the distress which this peace has done to the unfortunate Loyalists."[1]

It is usually said that about 100,000 of the 500,000 Loyalists left the U.S., but this figure seems much too high. Fairly "hard" but generous round figures for white emigrés indicate 45,000 in British North America, 10,000 in Great Britain, and about 5,500 in the islands, a total only slightly in excess of 60,000. The refugees were scattered far and wide throughout the islands. A few certainly reached Bermuda, the Virgin Islands, St. Kitts, Antigua, Montserrat, St. Vincent, St. Lucia, the Mosquito Shore, and doubtless several other locations. But their impact was slight, consisting mainly of the talents of a few outstanding individuals.

Only three places are habitually listed by the Admiralty as Loyalist havens that received substantial numbers plus the needed supplies and land-granting facilities. In ascending order of numerical importance they are: Dominica, perhaps 465; the Bahamas, about 2,000; Jamaica, over 3,000. Precise numbers will never be known. As a group the Loyalists brought about three times their number in slaves: 15,000 to the Bahamas and Jamaica, and a minimum of 450 to Dominica.

The island Loyalists came from all over America, but predictably the southern colonies contributed most heavily, especially South Carolina, then Georgia and North Carolina. Movement into the islands was sporadic, protracted and multi-routed, but the floodtides were the evacuation of Savannah and Charleston in 1782, the evacuation of New York during much of 1783, and the evacuation of East Florida from February 1783 until the end of 1785. Most Loyalists arrived on British government ships which one refugee, voicing a common gratitude, called "a great expense saved."[2] There is much evidence of the Loyalists characteristically moving around after arrival both within and between islands.

The impact of the Loyalists was most profound in the Bahamas where they perhaps doubled the white and almost quadrupled the black population. The number of white settlers may have dropped considerably, but it is certain that, at the least, the Loyalists almost equalled the old inhabitants *in toto,* and in some islands, including New Providence, Exuma and Cat Island, outnumbered them. Next in significance comes Dominica. This French island had been captured in 1761, was retaken in 1778 by Louis XVI, but returned to Britain by the peace treaty of 1783. Most of the 1,400 white inhabitants counted in 1782 were French, only 260 were British. So, while the 450 refugees could not hope to dominate, as in the Bahamas, they did greatly increase, and indeed outweigh, the existing British population which thereby became a more substantial minority. The Loyalists' slaves were not so important. Their number appears low, but even if we apply the three to one ratio, 1,350 is not a dramatic addition to the more than 13,000 slaves counted in 1782. The minimum 3,000 whites and 9,000 slaves in Jamaica are the greatest number, but had the least proportional impact. In 1785 the white population was 30,000 while slaves numbered 250,000.

On arrival in the islands, the condition of the refugees varied, but there were few who did not suffer from their exile. A typical exponential statement comes from Jamaica-bound James Carey who left behind in South Carolina "all his property that he could not carry off with him."[3] At one extreme this meant just a few bits of luggage, but in Carey's case destitution is not implied because the residue included fifty-six slaves. *The Cornwall Chronicle* of Montego Bay noted the arrival of another Loyalist with "a large quantity of valuable furniture, plate, china, and other effects."[4] A few lucky rich Loyalists in East Florida avoided selling their homes at depressed prices to the Spaniards by renting ships and transporting their dwellings in sections to the Bahamas. (Incidentally, some Loyalists' houses were similarly brought from Maine to New Brunswick.) More usually the refugees seem to have been "in the greatest distress," to quote a Jamaican.[5]

Initially, accommodation was the problem as Nassau, Kingston and Roseau, in particular, became extremely overcrowded. "There is not a house or shed to be got here to cover them, every place is full," cried the governor of Dominica, adding that until the Loyalists got land "they are incurring expenses which in a short time eat up all their little fortunes." Both private and public action was taken to alleviate conditions. The former seems to have included the running of a lottery in the Bahamas, while in Jamaica a committee raised money for charity including "a handsome sum" from the future William IV who made hopefully inspirational visits to several Loyalist havens.[6] By April 1783 it was reported all the Parishes of this Island had made "Generous Contributions" to the fund and that "about £3000" had been distributed "amongst the poorer sort."[7] In 1784, in Dominica, a similar committee began soliciting private charity.[8]

At the public level, as in British North America, the British government for some years provided rations, supplies and tools. There were widespread, probably exaggerated complaints of inadequacy from both refugees and local officials, but obviously anything was better than nothing, and in fact the aid was substantial.

The local legislatures adopted policies that the Jamaican Council described as its "most hospitable endeavours" to give the Loyalists "an Advantageous Asylum amongst us."[9] On March 1, 1783, an act was passed in Jamaica that exempted them for seven years from all public and parochial taxes (except quitrents), and from import taxes on their slaves, that freed them from all public service (except militia duty) and paid for the survey and patenting of all land grants. In Dominica the Assembly granted a fifteen-year exemption from all public taxes to the refugees and their slaves, and £1650 currency was voted for resettlement. In the Bahamas the Assembly was less generous, but the Loyalists were excused quitrents for 10 years.[10]

Land was the basis of survival for most Loyalists and as in British North America, Whitehall saw that free land was made available in the three islands. In the Bahamas, the Crown bought out the proprietors, in Jamaica and Dominica ungranted lands were distributed and in the latter some land owned by Frenchmen was gained through forfeiture or the expiration of leases.

Generally the history of Loyalist land-granting is one of bickering and complaint and, although it must not conceal much ultimate satisfaction, we must now note the negative side in Jamaica and Dominica. In Jamaica, a scandal developed over the Black River region of St. Elizabeth parish where 183 heads of families obtained land. Patrick Grant, the surveyor, claimed an exorbitant fee which, along with a Loyalist petition complaining about the poor quality of the land, sparked an enquiry by the House of Assembly during which it was suggested no "living creature, besides fish, frogs, Dutchmen, and amphibious animals, can exist in the district." But one local inhabitant went further, arguing that the land was "so unhealthy" that not even a frog could survive, which was proved by a Loyalist named Frogg who had left after losing "several of his family and slaves." The reference was to Robert Frogg, a tailor from Charleston, who returned to his trade in Kingston. This Black River land was and is a "morass," and despite hopes for rice production was, as the House concluded, "totally unfit for the purposes intended."[11] In Dominica, the governor himself said much of the available land was "not worth tilling," including that situated at Prince Rupert's Bay where some Loyalists forfeited their grants because unhealthy swamps prevented them making the required improvements.[12] Shades of Black River, but no mention of frogs— though "crapauds" were and are the Dominican national dish, as Loyalists at the time remarked.

Despite some carping, a Loyalist petition of 1787 in Dominica expressing satisfaction with "comfortable settlements" and "the fertility of the soil," and the frequent sincere use in Jamaica of epithets such as "this hospitable island" aptly expressed Loyalist attitudes. Generally the Colonial Office was quite successful in its avowed policy of affording the Loyalists "every possible Encouragement and Assistance."[13]

For a fortunate minority of refugees there were two other sources of relief: government compensation and government office. Many Loyalists with the expectation of compensation used it as security for loans with which they bought land and property, set themselves up as merchants or professionals. Sometimes the small amount awarded by the Claims Commissioners led to embarrassment. There was no equivalent in the islands to the creation of New Brunswick and with it a complete slate of new offices, but there were a few lucrative openings and some modest ones, particularly in the newly settled out-islands of the Bahamas. Thelma Peters concludes that usually the Loyalists served in unpaid positions— vestrymen, salt commissioners and the like.[14]

In assessing the life of the refugees we must consider the geographical characteristics of the islands. In contrast to the chilly lands of Canada there would be no freezing to death during the first winter. Several Loyalists—even some Northerners—deserted British North America for climatic reasons alone. The majority of Southerners never even considered going there, agreeing with

Governor Patrick Tonyn of East Florida that "Nova Scotia is too cold . . . for those who have lived in the southern colonies."[15] Southerners would not find climatic adjustment in the islands a problem. Northerners, though they might miss the winters, would not find Caribbean summers daunting because, as Samuel Quincy remarked, they were "no worse than Boston in the dog days."[16] Many island Loyalists agreed with the comment of William Wylly, the former speaker of the Georgia assembly, that those enjoying the Caribbean climate "cannot fail of being healthy."[17] but we must remember that the climate has only become entirely desirable with the modern conquest of tropical diseases. Several Loyalists did leave the islands for health reasons.

One scourge that afflicted the refugees in Jamaica was yellow fever which arrived in 1785, paradoxically from Philadelphia, but according to a Loyalist witness only "made great havoc . . . among newcomers and sailors." A modern scholar argues that at the time the Loyalists arrived "the conditions of mortality" were such that existing numbers of blacks and whites could only be maintained by "large-scale" immigration.[18]

An unpleasant feature of the Caribbean climate has always been hurricanes from which the Loyalists, like everyone else, suffered. Jamaica was particularly affected in the early years. Tropical storms struck in July 1784, August 1785 and October 1786 causing great suffering especially for the blacks because the destruction raised food prices. In August 1787 Dominica was the victim of a hurricane that caused eighty "desolated" Loyalists to petition for relief: "their buildings are torn to pieces, their growing crops . . . are entirely rooted out, beaten down and destroyed." The governor accordingly issued two months' rations. The Bahamas were also struck at that time, but generally were less affected by hurricanes, although two years earlier the storm of 1785 destroyed most of the islands' provisions, so that, according to Governor Powell, only government hand-outs prevented "starvation."[19]

On the positive side, the islands' climate provided an abundance of tropical fruit which was available cheap or even free. Today, a visit to the Bahamas in particular makes it difficult to believe that Loyalists who would eat fish could have gone hungry. They could readily harvest the "gardens of the sea," the "labyrinths of the coral grove where the purple mullet and the goldfish rove."[20] Those who tired of fish could turn to iguanas and turtles.

In the early eighteenth century Woods Rogers had complained that Bahamians lived "indolently," "fish being so plentiful." A Loyalist recalled that during her stay in Florida she got fat because of the "great abundance" of fish which was "our chief dependence and our ration." Of course, New Brunswick and Upper Canada were also "teeming" with fish (and, indeed, game), but the climate prevented much indolent living.[21]

For many Loyalists, including most of the well-to-do, the question of climate involved a single issue. As a group of them put it, a West India island "is the only place where they can employ their slaves to any advantage." Or as some Georgian Loyalists wrote to General Guy Carleton, they could not go North because of their Negroes "on whose labour the future subsistance [sic] of our families depends."[22] But before discussing the blacks, the whole question of the Loyalists' agricultural activities must be considered.

The climate of all the islands favored tropical fruits and allowed the growing of food crops at least at a subsistence level. Everywhere the Loyalists pursued stock raising, but again merely for subsistence. Samuel Quincy's complaint from Antigua was not uncommon: "no fine fresh butter, no changes of poultry, no wild geese, pheasant or duck, but good pork, beef, fish and fruit." In the Bahamas, at least, the thin pasturage encouraged sheep and goats rather than cattle.[23]

The Loyalists profoundly affected Bahamian agriculture. Schoepf (like Woods Rogers before him) found Conch agriculture primitive. There was too much reliance on the less demanding occupations of wrecking, wood-cutting and turtle and iguana hunting. A sharp stick was the most common agricultural tool. Lieutenant John Wilson, who surveyed the islands for the Loyalists, reported that although the Conchs had done little, the more industrious refugees would be able to grow corn and vegetables. Some individuals certainly were able to produce a diversity of provisions as a side line on their cotton plantations, but in general the Bahamas suffered shortages and became dependent on imports. For example, in 1789 one planter frantically requested provisions from Georgia simply to keep his slaves "alive." "For God's sake send us the corn at any freight."[24]

The great initial strength and eventual ruin of Bahamian Loyalist agriculture was cotton which rapidly became "a fascination" and a "mania," to quote a Loyalist and a modern historian respectively. As William Wylly put it in 1788, cotton growing "has infinitely exceeded our most sanguine expectations," so that even many merchants and professional men grew it as absentee proprietors. In 1790 *The Bahama Gazette,* noting the cotton boom, declared, "seven years since lands in the Bahamas were deemed of no value whatever. A fortunate reverse is now the case." The Loyalist, Joseph Eve, invented a cotton gin in 1793 which helped power the boom that also occurred in Barbados and elsewhere. For a time, seventy per cent of Britain's cotton imports came from the West Indies and even sugar was challenged as the chief crop. [25]

Decline came almost as fast as success. White gold turned to dross. By 1800 the cotton planters faced a ruin that was never reversed and was completely sealed by emancipation in 1834. The Bahamian soil was only superficially fertile. Soil exhaustion was worsened by poor husbandry. Natural setbacks included drought, cold weather, and most severe of all, the ravages of a devastating pest, the chenille bug, which elaborate control legislation by the House of Assembly in 1798 could not check. In 1802 a Society for the Propagation of the Gospel (S.P.G.) missionary reported "unhappy changes" and much emigration. [26] When Joseph Eve moved away in 1800, ginning soon disappeared because no one else could build or service the machines. Burton Williams, possibly the last surviving Loyalist, finished his life on the relic of his plantation on Watlings Island. He sagely dug his own grave, and when he died in 1834, the only tool a black servant could find with which to fill the hole was "a sharpened barrel stave," the classic pre-Loyalist Bahamian tool. [27]

Today, weather, termites and natural vegetation added to human retreat have left only a few ruins as testaments to the once prosperous plantation period. Cotton lingered on in a small way until this century, but is now of no more importance than when Columbus discovered the Bahamas.

In 1802 the Bahamas Agricultural Society was founded to offset the decline of cotton. It offered prizes for diversification, but to little avail. About the same time (although unconnected with the

Society) it appears that breadfruit was first cultivated successfully by a Loyalist, but it never gained the popularity it did in Jamaica. In 1806 the Society offered £1000 for the introduction of cochineal; in 1810 the government announced bounties on tar, pitch and turpentine, all without success. Ironically, agricultural initiative only paid off in the U.S. when in 1786 the growing of long- staple or Sea Island cotton was introduced to Georgia by a Loyalist planter named Roger Kelsall. It was, to quote Mathew Hammond, "the first event of importance . . . in the development of cotton culture in the United States." After 1790 the Southern States rapidly replaced the West Indies as Britain's chief supplier.[28]

Some Loyalists, and more often their slaves, remained on the plantations. But black and white alike converted to a Conch lifestyle: a patch of land for provisions, fishing, wrecking. As always, the Loyalists proved themselves good Americans—by the large number of mulatto children they sired and frequently manumitted. These offspring and the blacks in fact contributed more to the permanent settlement of the out-islands than did the whites.[29]

The Loyalist activities in Jamaican agriculture can only be glimpsed. Sugar, of course, had always been the prime Jamaican product and remained so. Many refugees may be presumed to have engaged in its production. In 1799 one wrote: "Perhaps the golden age of the planter has passed, but sugar must I think for some years bear a tolerable good price."[30] Coffee became a second staple just as most Loyalists began to arrive, and again we must presume that they took it up. One Loyalist, reporting his hurricane losses in 1784, listed—apart from a few acres of food supplies—about 1000 acres of coffee. Minor cash crops during the Loyalist period included limes, cotton, wool and indigo. A Loyalist wrote in 1784, "I have . . . [limes] growing upon my plantation in great abundance."[31] Cotton, a familiar if not yet major crop in Georgia and South Carolina, was not really suited climatically to Jamaica or the rest of the West Indies as it was to the Bahamas, but some Loyalists did grow it. Indigo was an important American crop and suited planters with a small slave force, but it suffered in Jamaica from a lack of the British bounties previously enjoyed in America. It was noted in January 1784 that immigrants were attracted to Jamaica by "the flattering accounts the [early] Loyalists there give of their crops of indigo.''[32] In August 1783 South Carolina and Georgia Loyalists in Jamaica, petitioning for a bounty, had noted, "the growth of Indigo is much more luxuriant in this Island than on the continent of North America.''[33] They added that its cultivation would open up the interior whence sugar was too heavy to transport. The conclusion is that indigo cultivation was stimulated by the Loyalists, but that it never attained serious importance. Several Loyalists announced their intention of growing rice and some probably succeeded, but again not on a large scale. Some corn was also raised. The disruption of the American Revolution including the arrival of the Loyalists created unfulfilled opportunities for diversification of the Jamaican economy. Frank Cundall, a leading Jamaican historian, claimed that between 1780 and 1787 about 15,000 blacks died because of lack of provisions.[34]

The Jamaican response to the Loyalists supports Edward Braithwaite's general, perhaps exaggerated, but valid conclusions regarding the islanders' reactions: they were conservative, "Creole," and unimaginative in character.[35]

In Dominica the assumption is that the Loyalists were satisfactorily assimilated into plantation and farming life. Coffee and sugar were the main cash crops before their arrival and remained so afterwards. These were unfamiliar crops to Americans and certainly some refugees did turn their hands to what they knew best. The government issue of "Indigo rakes" betokens the cultivation of that crop and the introduction of rice to the island is credited to the Loyalists.[36]

If evidence about the white Loyalists in the islands is skimpy, that about the blacks involved is skimpier still. The most incontrovertible and perhaps the most profound fact about the Loyalists in Jamaica and the Bahamas is that their slaves added substantially to the work force and that whatever the fate of the whites, the blacks' descendants are an important part of the present population of the islands.

Part of the Loyalists' motivation for coming was the need for slave employment. Several large slave owners, who never went themselves, sent portions of their slave holdings to Jamaica where opportunities for "jobbing" and public works employment were readily available. The old white inhabitants and Loyalists discovered many differences between themselves and the same was true of blacks, especially when the Americans had been born into or lived long under a system that could be more educational. According to the Reverend George W. Bridges, an early nineteenth century historian of Jamaica, the Loyalists brought with them not only "fixed principles" but also "faithful slaves, who were much further advanced on the scale of civilized society than the plantation negroes, amongst whom they were here dispersed, and over whom their example soon spread its beneficial influence." For Bridges, who was almost insanely committed to the planters' cause, this example was a happy acceptance of the benefits of slavery.[37] Some decades ago Mrs. Maxfield Parrish, who lived for many years in Nassau while writing a book on Negro folk songs in the U.S., was struck by the popularity of many of the same songs in the Bahamas, which suggested strong black American cultural influences.[38]

In the Bahamas, the arrival of the Loyalists' slaves caused the whites to be outnumbered for the first time. The result was a tightening of control. The Loyalists engineered a stricter slave code, set up the militia as a precaution and initiated night patrols. The disarray of the evacuations from the colonies and the existence of blacks who had earned their freedom by fighting for the British caused confusion marked by much litigation over ownership. Many Loyalists claimed slaves (some of whom were stolen from patriots) whom they did not legally own; others enslaved those who were legally free. In 1786 an official reported from New Providence that "it is with great Pain of Mind that I, every day, see the Negroes, who came here from America, with the British General's Free Papers, treated with unheard of cruelty, by Men who call themselves Loyalists. Those unhappy People after being drawn from their Masters by Promises of Freedom, and the King's Protection, are every day stolen away from this Island, shipped, and disposed of to the French at Hispaniola." Slaves were desperately sought because they counted in the distribution of land and supplies, could be used as collateral for loans and, of course, were a means to economic success.

Nothing like the Maroon uprisings of Jamaica and Dominica are found in the Bahamas, but by 1787 Governor Dunmore was complaining of "Outrages" committed by runaways who, he admitted, included disgruntled black ex-soldiers and freemen now enslaved.[40] A general pardon defused the situation and the institution of slavery seems to have been comparatively benign, if we can believe the comments of Schoepf (1784), McKinnon(1803) or the celebrated *Journal* (1831-32) of Farquarson.[41] Of course benignness was stimulated when many owners began to find their slaves a liability. It was claimed by Mrs. Parrish that the Bahamian colour line did not harden until the rise of American tourism marked by the construction of the splendid Royal Victoria Hotel in 1859. Nevertheless, in the islands most Loyalists were alarmed by the growing British emancipation movement. Illegal slave trading after 1807 sparked a famous constitutional rumpus in the Bahamas Assembly (1816-20) with William Wylly representing a minority pro-Black view as the victim. Most Loyalists probably agreed with a Jamaican who said in 1788: "What will those who read the History of George the third 50 years hence [think] that within the course of 12 years the King and People of England first wanted to make slaves of their own Free Subjects in America—that not being accomplished and losing a mighty empire—a *similar* frenzy took them, and they wanted to make *Slaves Free*— good by to your Colonies if you pass such a Law."[42]

One might expect most black Loyalists to have avoided the Caribbean for British North America, though as it turned out there they also got a raw deal. But a few free blacks did reach the islands, usually as members of Loyalist regiments. Jamaica received a substantial number of black Loyalists by the evacuation of Savannah and particularly Charleston, including five hundred members of Dunmore's black regiment and a black South Carolina corps. By the latter evacuation, St. Lucia gained a ship load of "Black Pioneers." Another regiment ended up in Grenada. The evacuation of New York included the dispatch of a number of free blacks to Abaco Island in the Bahamas.[43]

The presence of the South Carolina black soldiers raised apprehensions in Jamaica of "their being turned loose here" and the effect the example would have on slaves. To the whites' relief the regiment was shipped to the Leeward Islands and continued its service to the king during the French Wars.[44]

At this point, a footnote on another maligned minority—the Indians. The Six Nations were a major force in Northern Loyalism, and in the South to a lesser degree the McGillivray family and Col. Thomas Brown kept the Creks fairly loyal, while John Stuart played a similar role among the Cherokees. Joseph Brant was encouraged to lead his followers into "Canada," but the British authorities were not keen on a similar exodus of Southern "Indian friends" to the islands. Nevertheless, a small colony of Creek emigrés was formed on the outskirts of Nassau. Another interesting North-South parallel is that just as the British, partly because of Indian considerations, kept control of forts in the old Northwest after the peace treaty, so southern interests in the Bahamas tried to maintain themselves in the Floridas where two Nassau-based, partly Loyalist, trading companies—Panton, Leslie and Company and Miller, Bonnamy and Company—competed. The former had Spanish support which drove the latter, abetted by Governor Dunmore, to launch an abortive filibuster led by a Maryland Loyalist, William Bowles, which ambitiously sought to establish a Loyalist state on the southern mainland. A few disgruntled Loyalists were persuaded by Bowles to leave the Bahamas in 1787 and settle in New Smyrna under the Spanish government. The tragic third act to a drama whose first act was Deveaux's capture of New Providence launched from Florida in 1783, was a filibuster during the war of 1812 that saw the execution by General Andrew Jackson of Robert Chrystie Armbrister, the son of a Charleston Loyalist, and Alexander Arbuthnot, a Bahamian merchant. This incident produced a bitterness towards the U.S. amongst the Loyalists comparable to that engendered in Upper Canada during the same war.[45]

Internal conflict is a normal characteristic amongst refugees and the white Loyalists were no exception. During the Revolution they had quarreled with the British commanders and with each other almost as much as with the rebels. In the islands, they quarreled bitterly with each other over land grants, office, slave-ownership and later over emancipation. In the Bahamas, Robert Rumer's charge that Andrew Deveaux was unfairly taking all the credit for the Loyalist capture of New Providence from the Spanish presaged a major political division involving Governor John Maxwell. In 1784 General Alexander McArthur reported near-civil war among the Abaco Loyalists at the new Loyalist town of Carleton (probably the present Hopetown). Troops had to be brought in and a group of dissident Tories moved away to form the rival settlement of Marsh Harbour. On the other hand, the refugees were typically clannish. They frequently settled in groups that had blood, economic and social ties reaching back to their days on the mainland. An example from South Carolina is a cluster of Wilkins and Kelsall families on Little Exuma. A bizarre result of clannishness, admittedly involving intermarriage with the Conchs, was found in 1903 by an American scientific expedition to Hopetown which discovered a forlorn, poverty-stricken colony of Loyalist descendants who had maintained their racial purity at the cost of a horrifying inbreeding that had produced idiots, dwarfs and various diseases and physical deformities. The one thousand white inhabitants of Hopetown were almost all descendants of one person, Wyannie Malone, a Loyalist lady who had fled from South Carolina in 1785.[46]

The refugees tended to be drawn together by common enemies; usually the old inhabitants (such as the Blue Noses of Nova Scotia) and the British authorities (such as Governor Parr's regime in the same colony). A most dramatic example occurred in the Bahamas. Historians and disinterested contemporaries share the Loyalists' low opinion of the pre-Loyalists. Schoepf called the Conchs "amiable" but idle, they lacked drive and initiative; a Conch fortune "consisted in a piano and a pair of night shades!"[47] The S.P.G. missionaries made some telling comments. One reported from Exuma that the Conchs there were poor, almost illiterate, unchurched and given over to swearing and drinking. The Loyalists were much better educated, but in the *wrong* way; "the gentry . . . employ their leisure hours in reading the works of Manderille, Gibbon, Voltaire, Rousseau and Hume." Another missionary added that the Loyalists were "unhappily . . . brought up in the Northern school of modern politics."[48] Symbolically in 1790 the Loyalists in the Bahamian House of Assembly tried to purchase "the Silver Mace of the late Assembly of the Province of South Carolina." Also symbolically in Nassau the registry office books became dramatically better kept when the Loyalists, Adam Chrystie and his assistant, James Armbrister, took over.[49]

In 1785 a Nassau grand jury dominated by Loyalists drew up a list of grievances that amounted to a massive criticism of the Conchs. The complaints concerned lack of fire-fighting equipment and garbage disposal, lack of an adequate jail and poor house, lack of discipline among blacks, failure to maintain cemeteries properly, failure to control tippling houses and cooking fires near wooden buildings, and too high a duty on tea.[50]

Two different societies were in a conflict that was partly an echo of the traditional enmity between Creoles and Europeans. To this must be added the threatening number of Loyalists and their arrogance which led them to behave as if Deveaux had not only defeated the Spaniards but also the old inhabitants.

In addition to the usual dissatisfaction with resettlement and the granting of land, rioting against the crews of American ships in Nassau harbor broke out in the summer of 1784. Like Governor Parr in Nova Scotia, Governor Maxwell favored the old inhabitants and disliked the Loyalists who, he complained, "almost wish to take over the government." The Loyalist, Stephen Haven received the following outburst: "God damn me Sir! You want to engraft Augustine Customs, Governors, Lawyers, Staff and all upon us." The refugees, led by James Hepburn of North Carolina, organized themselves against the governor forming a Board to "preserve and maintain these Rights and Liberties for which they have left their homes and their possessions." A quasi-revolutionary situation developed and Maxwell was recalled to England in February 1785.[51]

It must be added that the Loyalists were not entirely united against Maxwell. He had some Loyalist support from the West Florida and humble refugees in general who did not particularly like the merchant-planter elite. Even some of the latter supported him, including Alexander Ross who was originally a member of the Loyalist Board, Thomas Roker from Pennsylvania, who became Speaker of the House, and John O'Halloran, an Assemblyman, originally from South Carolina.

Maxwell's successor was a Georgia Loyalist, James Edward Powell, but conditions did not at first improve. Powell inherited a new assembly that was sharply divided. The Loyalist members, who numbered at least nine, claimed they had been deprived of a

majority in the twenty-five seat house by the illegal actions of the
Provost Marshal of New Providence. Conversely, the old inhabitants claimed Loyalist gerrymandering on Andros Island. The
upshot was a boycott by most of the Loyalist members of what they
called an " *illegally* chosen" body. In April 1785 the Common
Hangman publicly burned a Loyalist protest, and in early May a
Loyalist meeting denied the legitimacy of any "laws the Asembly
might pass" and called for new elections. Again, the situation was
becoming quasi-revolutionary. In September, eight Loyalist
radicals were expelled from the House. The "Long Parliament" of
the Bahamas was not to be dissolved until 1794 and the Loyalists
seemed vanquished, but in fact they gradually asserted control,
winning every by-election but one. Powell and his successor, John
Brown, proved to be healing forces, while a temporary economic
prosperity added to the calm.[52]

However, the arrival of Lord Dunmore as governor in October
1787 inaugurated both economic and political depression. Dunmore, as last royal governor of Virginia was, as the fiasco at the
Great Bridge had already shown, the kind of friend the Loyalists
were better off without. During his inept "reign" he favored the
Conchs to a degree and the opposition was fittingly led by William
Wylly. After a long controversy the Assembly permanently asserted
its control over the Bahamas budget. Again the Loyalists had
proved themselves good Americans. A general election in 1794
resulted in Loyalist control. In 1796 Dunmore was replaced by a
Loyalist, John Forbes, and the critical political period was at an
end. Loyalist ascendancy was symbolized by the erection between
1803 and 1812 of the still extant, elegant public buildings housing
the Assembly, Council and Court that were modelled on similar
structures in New Bern, North Carolina.

The political history of the Loyalists indicates that they, no less
than the rebels, were educated and radicalized by the American
Revolution. Their attacks on Maxwell and Dunmore were uncan-
nily reminiscent of those of the patriots. "An American Loyalist,"
writing in *The Bahama Gazette* (April 2, 1785), asked the Old Inhabitants to "repudiate the governor" and "to emancipate themselves from the thraldom of a few placemen and Dependents."[53]

Nothing comparable to the Bahamian political disturbances can be found in Dominica or Jamaica. Governor Orde of Dominica, like Dunmore, was no stranger to America or the Loyalists, having served in the Royal Navy in South Carolina and having married a Charleston girl. He was well disposed towards the refugees and did his best for them. He faced serious problems with his mainly old French inhabitants who were sullenly antagonistic to restored British rule and were disliked by the English minority. He also had to contend with the serious maraudings of a "Legion" of Maroons. Orde seems to have handled these problems well and indeed was awarded a baronetcy for putting down the black rebels. He did quarrel a lot with the Assembly, but the Loyalists do not seem to have been specifically involved. In 1791, following charges by some Dominicans, an enquiry was made by the Privy Council into the governor's distribution of supplies to Loyalists. The charges were dismissed as "frivolous."[54] The full story of this episode is not entirely clear, but I do not think it arose out of any old inhabitant versus Loyalist or Loyalist versus Governor conflict.

In Jamaica, although Governor Sir Alured Clarke called the Loyalists "very importunate," both he and his predecessor, Archibald Campbell, were favourably disposed to them, a possible reflection of their experiences as commanders during the Revolutionary war.[55]

There were no rifts in the Jamaica Assembly such as wrecked the Bahamas. This was partly because of the lack of Loyalist political power—probably only one or two Loyalists ever reached the House of Assembly or the Kingston Vestry. As already noted, Surveyor Grant's activities in St. Elizabeth parish were investigated by the House, but this reflected concern for the Loyalists, not antagonism. However, some antagonism did indeed exist. The clearest example is the protest by the old inhabitants of the Parish of Kingston, where the majority of Loyalists resided, against the tax exemption act which the parish unsuccessfully sought to have repealed. The Kingston vestry approved the principle of helping the Loyalists, but in practice the law had been "very detrimental" to them for two rather opposing reasons. On the one hand, many of the exempted Loyalists "are apparently wealthy and practice commerce to a considerable extent; many tradesmen or mechanics are in the exercise of lucrative employment . . ., and many of the houses they inhabit are elegant and in some of the best situations, in town.'' The vestry saw opportunism and even chicanery by ''specious'' Loyalists—''many traders, who neither by compulsion or otherwise, abandoned any real property, or lost anything by the revolution, but became passive to the spirit of the times, and transported themselves with their effects, to this town, as a more eligible situation for their business.'' Wealthy Loyalists were enjoying all the advantages of Jamaican society without any of the expenses. On the other hand and even worse, the loss of revenue caused by tax exemption was particularly ill-timed because of the cost of supporting ''numerous poor'' Loyalists, ''destitute of the necessities of life, and wholly unable, in this climate, to earn their subsistence.'' Some were in the overcrowded parish house, others received ''Outpensions,'' others had been shipped elsewhere, usually to the U.S. or Britain at great parochial expense. Other complaints included the generally bad economic times, inter-marriage and the fact that the privileged Loyalists were competing for the dwindling trade of the island.[56]

There are other hints of tension. Patrick Grant noted that some of the inhabitants opposed Loyalist settlement on the morass because it would deprive them of pasturage during the dry season. An old inhabitant complained that certain ''Wretches'' had ''decoy'd'' slaves from the Loyalists. Only one refugee is recorded as finding Jamaican society depraved, the Sabbath profaned, ''morals . . . at the lowest ebb,'' but the feeling was probably more widespread.[57]

As the history of contemporary displaced persons the world over suggests—from Hungarians in Britain in the late 1950s to the present Vietnamese in the U.S.—it would have been a miracle if the arrival of the Loyalists at their various locations had not caused friction. The Loyalists were Americans, and neither the islands nor London nor Halifax were America. ''I do not like the place, or the Inhabitants, near so well as Carolina,'' murmured one on arrival in Jamaica.[58]

Signs are that if the Loyalists had come to Jamaica in numbers as large as they did to the Bahamas a similarly bitter quarrel would have ensured.

The Loyalists contributed significantly to the literary life of

Jamaica, the Bahamas and possibly Dominica. About 1771 young Alexander Aikman emigrated from Scotland to Charleston, South Carolina, where he was apprenticed to Robert Wells, another Scottish immigrant who was a distinguished loyal bookseller and printer of *The South Carolina Gazette.* At the beginning of the Revolution Aikman fled, ending up in Jamaica where in 1778 he began the *Jamaica Mercury* which became *The Royal Gazette* two years later. In 1799 he founded a second newspaper in Spanish Town. For many years he was printer to the King and the House of Assembly and for many terms sat in that House for the parish of St. George. In 1782 in Kingston, he married Louisa S. Wells, the daughter of his former master. Their son, Alexander Jr., succeeded his father in the two official printing positions.[59]

Frank Cundall wrote that Alexander Aikman Sr. the island's leading publisher, "did more than any one else in cause of printing" in Jamaica, and judged the twelve volumes of the Journals of the House of Assembly printed by Aikman between 1797 and 1816 as "the most elaborate and important piece of printing undertaken in the colony, then or since," adding, "As a work of typography it has never been surpassed in Jamaica, and bears comparison with typographical work of the period anywhere." Aikman's brother, William, fled to Jamaica in 1775 and until his death in 1784 was a valuable addition to the life of Kingston where he opened a "Book and Stationery Store" in King Street. He entered into a printing partnership with David Douglass. Douglass, the founder of the famous American Company of Comedians, was a notable Loyalist addition to Jamaica where he became Master of the Revels. I have not yet discovered exactly what his theatrical accomplishments were in the island, but he prospered greatly and was certainly in the printing business until his death in Spanish Town in 1786.[60]

The Wells family is very interesting. One of Louisa's brothers, Dr. William C. Wells, published the first newspaper in Florida between 1782 and 1784. He then fled to Britain and had a distinguished career as a leading intellectual, medical doctor and author. In August 1784 another brother, John Wells, began the first newspaper in the Bahamas, *The Bahama Gazette,* an excellent organ, the greatest Loyalist cultural contribution to the islands, which circulated throughout the Bahamas as well as Charleston,

Savannah and Bermuda. Its masthead bore Horace's words, *Nullius Addictus Jurare in Verba Magistri*—"not bound in loyalty to any masters"—a fitting token of the Loyalists' good Americanism and lack of Toryism both at home and New Providence. By carrying both pro- and anti-Maxwell material, the *Gazette* lived up to Horace's philosophy. William Wells had employed the same slogan for the *East Florida Gazette* as had the father, Robert Wells, in South Carolina. It is pleasant to remark that today the *Nassau Daily Tribune* is still using the motto. Thus, one definite Loyalist tradition lives.[61]

Like his father John Wells opened a book and stationery store (the only one in Nassau) and published various things including the *Bahama Almanack*. There were two other Loyalist printers. The previously mentioned mini-Franklin, Joseph Eve, was for a time printer to the House of Assembly, and a second, hitherto lost, Nassau paper, *The Lucayan Royal Herald* was founded by Alexander Cameron, a Virginia Loyalist.

Incredibly, there were three English newspapers in Dominica during the Loyalists' era. John Lowndes, who published one of them, the *Charibbean Register; or, Ancient and Original Dominica Gazette,* was almost certainly from South Carolina and probably a Loyalist.

In the Bahamas, if nowhere else, there were important Loyalist contributions beyond agriculture and printing. Several Loyalists, including some on Ragged Island, successfully followed the traditional Conch occupation of salt-raking which nicely complemented cotton growing because when harvesting ended in early Spring, the slaves could be moved out to the salt ponds.[62]

According to William Wylly, the Loyalists spectacularly increased the number of merchants in New Providence from three to twenty-six. This assertion is backed up by Thelma Peters who wrote: "Probably no small city in the world had more merchants than Nassau after the coming of the Loyalists." Obviously there was an over-abundance. Some moved successfully to the out-islands, some turned to planting and a few got government jobs. Some of those who persisted in trade, such as William Alexander, William Panton and Thomas Forbes of the firm of Panton, Leslie and Company, prospered. Others survived, but in reduced cir-

cumstances. Thus Roger Kelsall, a former member of a loyal mercantile community in Sunbury, Georgia, lamented in his will in
1788, "If my estate fall short impute it to no fault of mine, but to
the inevitable misfortune . . . of the late most accurs'd
rebellion."[63]

Shipbuilding utilizing local wood was given a fillip by Loyalist
shipbuilders and their skilled slave shipwrights. For example, in
early 1786 William Begbie and Daniel Manson from South
Carolina launched the 300-ton *Polly,* the largest ship ever built in
the Bahamas to that date.[64]

The Loyalists increased and sometimes began settlement in
many Bahamian islands, but the most striking transformation occurred in Nassau. Schoepf noted a primitive Nassau consisting of
"but one tolerably regular street, or line of houses, which runs next
the water." With the influx of refugees, new streets and houses appeared, the latter boasting such novelties as basements.[65]

A shed "under the splended name of *Bourse*" was replaced
about 1787 with the elegant Vendue House, now the headquarters
of the Bahamas Electricity Corporation; the decaying cemeteries
were improved; Joseph Eve designed and built St. Mathew's, "the
oldest extant church"; the docks were upgraded; a poor house, a
new jail (now the charming octagonal library) and the other public
buildings around Parliament Square were constructed. In short,
Nassau assumed its modern character. One can add the beginning
of the police force, improved fire protection—a fire engine was
brought from Florida—the founding of several private schools, including one presided over by David Zubly of the famous Georgia
Loyalist family, a lending library containing 500 volumes and the
introduction of both amateur and professional theatricals. The
cultural loss to the Young Republic has often been speculated upon
and is confirmed by the inventories of some Loyalists' estates. For
example, John Kelsall, son of Robert Kelsall, left a large collection
of books in 1806.[6]

It seems likely that Kingston, Jamaica, where so many Loyalists
settled, received a similar, but minor boost. The Jamaica
Almanack for 1785 reported that although a great fire in 1782 had
consumed over eighty houses, "most of them are now rebuilt, and
other parts of the town are filling up fast, the number of buildings

in 1785 will much exceed that of any former year." At least one Loyalist, John Ross from North Carolina, was a shipbuilder, and James Broglie operated a foundry at Morant Bay.[67]

Any discussion of the impact of the Loyalists must note not only outstanding individuals, but also must attempt a mass analysis. Space precludes considering an analysis made by Thelma Peters of the eighty families studied by Mrs. Parrish and an analysis I have made of one hundred and ten refugees who were granted special certificates of loyalty in Jamaica, but I will mention one theme: the recurring division between rich and poor that was epitomized in Saint John, New Brunswick, by the famous election fight in 1784 between Upper Covers and Lower Covers. John Graham, the former lieutenant-governor of Georgia, reported that the evacuations of Savannah and Charleston had brought 4,000 white Loyalists to East Florida. About half were accompanied by a total of at least 5,000 slaves salvaged "from the wrecks of their fortunes"; the other half were mainly small back country farmers from South Carolina and Georgia who had owned "few or no Negroes" and had arrived propertyless. The former would have to go to the islands "where only they can employ their Negroes, or reap any benefit from such property"; the latter ought to go to Nova Scotia but because of the climate probably would not. Graham recommended the Bahamas "where I have been credibly informed they may without labour of Negroes earn a Comfortable Subsistence." Abaco and the northern part of Eleuthera, which have a much cooler climate than the southern Bahamas, almost from the beginning proved unfitted for plantation life. Here the humble Loyalists, who unlike the slave-owners and merchants did not antagonize the Conchs, intermarried with them, adapted to their way of life based on the sea and established several settlements, particularly on the off-shore islands of Northern Abaco, including Marsh Harbour, Hopetown, and New Plymouth Town which was the most successful and still thrives. The name suggests the northern origin of some of the settlers and even today the way of life and geography are reminiscent of New England. One might add that Maxwell distinguished between the humble Loyalists whom he liked and the rest whom he detested. Governor Powell called the poorer sort "Arabs" and erroneously doubted if they could survive.[68]

Although evidence concerning the socio-economic characteristics of the Loyalists who reached Dominica is sketchy, the low estimates of the number of slaves they brought does not suggest outstanding wealth. Orde described one group of twenty or thirty as "of low degree" and a member of the Council said on the arrival of another eighty-five that they "were not then nor ever have been in Affluent Circumstances and some of them really indigent." Among the tools distributed were those for blacksmiths, coopers, sawyers, and shipwrights, though it is likely that some of these implements were intended for the use of Loyalists' slaves.[69]

In Jamaica a division between rich and poor has already been indicated by the complaints of the Kingston vestry.

Despite some solid, and in the Bahamas even spectacular, contributions the Loyalists' impact on the islands was disappointing, often ephemeral. Today they are practically forgotten in Jamaica, and in Dominica a leading citizen reports that "emigration and intermarriage have swept away all trace" of them.[70] This raises the still unanswered question of how many Loyalists moved away. As in New Brunswick, the movement was certainly important. In all the islands the whites, including the Loyalists and their descendants, were encouraged to leave because of poor land, hurricanes, the failure to re-open trade with the United States—policies, as Bridges put it, entirely "in favour of the local interests of Canada[71]—the dislocation of the French wars, and most profoundly by emancipation. The arrival of the Loyalists unfortunately for them coincided with what Professor Ragatz called "the critical period in British West Indian history witnessing the . . . transition from . . . a commanding position to ruin and stagnation."[72]

Of all the islands the Bahamas were the most permanently influenced by the Loyalists. The shape of Nassau and the extension of settlement have already been mentioned. Loyalist descendants are still prominent today in some places such as Bay Street, Long Island (which in 1937 was claimed to have the greatest concentration)[73] and, of course, Abaco where the Loyalist inheritance sparked a secessionist threat when independence and black power came in 1973.[74] One can add the indisputable contribution of place names, such as Lyford Cay, after William Lyford of Georgia.[75]

Loyalist traditions still live, if not quite as vigorously as might be expected. But even in the Bahamas, the Loyalist thrust was blunted. I have already noted the ruins of the collapsed cotton plantations. Similarly the cultural thrust was not sustained; thus, although the *Gazette* was still being published in 1824, a visitor reported that "books are not to be purchased; there are no bookstores."[76] The waning of Loyalist influence was certainly affected by migration. Many failing planters left the out-islands for New Providence or moved out of the Bahamas completely, often to the U.S. In the second half of the nineteenth century, another important loss was sustained when many Abacoan wreckers, hurt by the building of lighthouses, settled in Florida.[77] The extent of Loyalist retreat is disputed by historians. Talbot Bethel and Michael Craton play it down; Paul Albury and Mrs. Parrish stress it.[78]

The Loyalists who so often came from the peripheries of the thirteen colonies as often fled to the peripheries of the British empire (New Brunswick, Upper Canada, Sierra Leone and the Bahamas) or to newly conquered areas (Quebec and Dominica). Great Britain and Jamaica were not peripheral in themselves but often proved so for the refugees. As so often in the history of colonization, seemingly more attractive areas (here the islands) proved less productive and permanent than the forbidding ones (here British North America). In both places it was generally not the elite but the rank and file who contributed most by simply opening up the land. Their lack of capital, education and high expectations saved them from the lure of cotton planting, aristocratic estate-building and office seeking.

I arrived for the first time in Nassau in 1973 two days after the Prince of Wales presided over the granting of Bahamian independence. I was struck by the great number of familiar names in the newspaper which I naively took to belong to the Loyalists' descendants. Most of course, were actually the descendants of the slaves of Loyalists. Thus the Loyalist influence does continue in a more wholesome form than the Bay Street oligarchy. It is a legacy that I like to think the Loyalists themselves, at their best, would approve.

BERMUDA IN 1776:
LOYALIST—OR JUST NEUTRAL?

BY

ESMOND WRIGHT

═══════════════════

IT is natural to generalize about the West Indian islands, in 1776 as today, as if they were a single place. They were, and are, very diverse. The Bermudas, in particular, do not fit easily into any pattern that holds for the rest. They comprise a number of small islands 500 miles to the east of North Carolina and cover some twenty square miles. The largest—Great Bermuda, or Main Island—is fourteen miles by one; northeast of it and forming a semicircle round Castle Harbor are the rest of the group, including St. George. This port could accommodate a large fleet and was the only Bermuda port authorized under the Navigation Acts; to it therefore all shipping had by law to go. Naturally enough, it was in St. George real estate that local men of property invested.

The islands, known frequently in North America at the time as the Summer or more accurately the Somers Islands, acquired the name of Bermuda from the shipwreck of Juan Bermudez, a Spaniard on a voyage from Spain to Cuba who was wrecked there. The first settlement was begun by Sir George Somers in 1609, but in 1612 the islands were granted to an offshoot of the Virginia Company and some sixty people under Henry More settled there. They cultivated tobacco, but the industry gradually declined in the 18th

99

century. In 1774 the population of the Bermudas was estimated by Governor Bruere at 10,655—almost equally divided between whites and blacks.[1] They lived by sloop-building—many American privateers were Bermuda-built—by smuggling and privateering, and after 1776, by trading openly and shamelessly with the mainland colonies.[2]

The situation in the Bermudas in 1776 was a particularly involved one. Their geographical location and poverty prevented their becoming a major refugee center for Loyalists.

In population they were small, and equally divided between whites and blacks, unlike Jamaica's ten to one black/white ratio. If they had their own black risings, as in 1761, they were much less serious, and there was indeed a dependence of black on white and white on black very different from that in Jamaica. Governor Bruere found it "a kind of paradise by nature but without art, cultivation or agriculture, and with little regulation or order." But he was soon to add references to "the supineness and indolence of the inhabitants."[3] Agriculture on the Bermudas consisted almost exclusively of subsistence farming; meat and even fish were usually scarce; pilfering was a major occupation. From their great asset the cedar tree they constructed a hardy seagoing sloop for the carrying trade. In the years of war prosperity up to 1763 they were building 35 sloops a year.

The Bermudians built up a triangular trade: salt from the Turks and Tortuga and logwood to Britain; cloth and hardware to the mainland colonies, and provisions for themselves, a trade employing 1000.[4] The largest shipper on the islands was Jennings, Tucker & Co., who traded regularly to London and the mainland, and the two families were dominant politically and socially. Since the islands were well endowed with creeks, inlets and harbors, smuggling was rife and difficult to check. So indeed were wrecking and salvaging. A contingent of regular troops—the Ninth Regiment or Royal Norfolks—had been brought in but, located in St George's, could easily be evaded, and in 1768 were transferred to cope with the situation in North America. The two detachments in Bermuda and the Bahamas were recalled to St. Augustine where the regiment was. From that point on the sole defence of the island was left in the hands of the local militia.

The Association devised by the first Continental Congress in 1774 threatened the Bermudas severely and they faced starvation. A delegation led by Colonel Henry Tucker visited Philadelphia in 1776 to ask that the islands be supplied with necessities. Colonel Tucker's was a difficult, though for many of his contemporaries, not an unusual, role. His eldest son was a Bermuda councillor and had three years before married Frances, the Governor's daughter. His second son was a physician in South Carolina. His third, once clerk of the Bermuda Council, was studying medicine at Edinburgh. His fourth, St. George, was studying law at William and Mary and was so strongly patriot in inclination that his anxious father—pleading economy—brought him back. It was indeed the Tucker family which helped to remove the powder at St. George's and ship it to Charleston and Philadelphia in August 1775, to the Governor's indignation and alarm. As a result the Continental Congress on 22 November 1775, after spending a whole day in committee of the whole discussing the island's needs, agreed "that the Inhabitants of the Island of Bermuda appear friendly to the cause of America, and ought to be supplied with . . . the produce of these colonies . . . necessary for their subsistence and home consumption." It voted that they should be permitted to import annually from the colonies 72,000 bushels of Indian corn, 2,000 barrels of bread or flour, 1,000 barrels of beef or pork, 21,000 bushels of peas or beans, and 300 tierces of rice. This was to be an annual supply and to be allocated among various colonies. For the immediate needs of the Bermudians, the Congress further voted that a cargo of provisions should be sent in the brig *Sea Nymph* commanded by Captain Samuel Stobel. The people of Bermuda were delighted with "this concession" made by the Continental Congress, however unwilling they were to bid open defiance to the power of Great Britain. Under the circumstances, Governor Bruere felt himself isolated and was doubtless confirmed in the feelings he had expressed at an earlier date when he wrote to the Earl of Dartmouth that he could not "confide in any person here, at present," as there seemed to be "few friends of government here." W.G. Kerr in his *Bermuda and the American Revolution* describes the situation thus:

> Twenty sail of Bermuda vessels, nominally engaged in
> picking up wrecks and turtles at the Bahama banks, sold
> the revolting colonists ships, salt, cannon and military
> stores, thus keeping in supplies the American privateers
> who preyed on the West India trade. In fact, most
> American privateering ships were Bermuda-built. The
> salt makers at Turks Island did a lively trade, exchang-
> ing their produce for flour and grain."[5]

The geographical position of the Bermudas and their small
population made any alternative strategy for them impossible.
Their tacit relationship with the colonies as essentially an economic
supplier—not least (once war began) of salt—and a suppliant, was
occasionally interrupted by the appearance of British warships. In
November 1778 however a British garrison of two companies arrived under the command of Major William Sutherland, reinforced
in December 1779 by an additional 100 men under Lieut-Col.
Donkin; from then on the colony was under British protection and
control. Many of the leading figures however traded openly with
the enemy. After 1780 there were frequent expectations of French
or Spanish invasion—and even of Bermuda becoming openly
"rebellious." In 1781 St. George Tucker wrote to Washington:

> The reduction of Bermuda would open again those
> resources for the supply of salt to the Continent, the
> obstruction of which has been severely felt by the in-
> habitants of [Virginia] in particular, who not being fur-
> nished with vessels of their own, have been obliged to
> depend on the fortuitous arrival of Bermudians driven
> hither by necessity, or allured by the advantages of our
> commerce, to brave even the horrors of a prison-ship,
> which many of them have fatally experienced. A capitu-
> lation nearly similar to that of Grenada would ensure
> this end . . . I would presume that a fifty-gun ship and
> three or four frigates with some land forces would ac-
> complish this end in no less than three days, there being
> no garrison in the place except about 300 invalids.

Later, in detail, he advised that Castle Harbor and St George's
Harbor be entered and the blow struck from within. If this proved

impossible, then a force should be landed at Tucker's Town to reduce the Castle, and another at Ferry Point to overpower the town and fortifications at St. George's.

Washington was sufficiently interested for Tucker to elaborate the plan over many pages, suggesting that the whole scheme be considered by "some respectable gentleman" resident at the West End. He knew of competent pilots who were available and thought the time suitable for action; and, he continued, in the event of success Bermuda could remain a neutral island until the end of the war when a disposition of it could be made in accordance with the wish of its own people and the best interests of the United States and her allies.

A number of Virginians, some of them exotic, can clearly be identified as early refugees in Bermuda. According to Dunmore's letter to Germain of July 31 1776, some of his followers were then about to sail for Great Britain, others for the West Indies, and still others for St. Augustine in East Florida. According to a letter written by one of the passengers on the same date, those on board the ship *Logan* were going to Glasgow, Scotland, while other vessels were bound for the English ports, London and Whitehaven, and still others for St. Augustine and the island of Antigua. Strangely enough, Staten Island, New York, which was the immediate destination of Dunmore himself and about a thousand other refugees, white and black, was not mentioned by either writer; nor was Bermuda, which was not at that time always distinguished from the other West Indian Islands.

A few Virginia families did go to Bermuda. Among these were Samuel Farmer and his household, except his eldest son who sailed first to New York, then to the West Indies in October 1778, and year later to Bermuda, where his father died in May, 1780. Robert Shodden, the merchant of Portsmouth, with his wife and two children, also sailed for Bermuda accompanied or followed by Mrs Shodden's brothers, William and Bridger Goodrich. Bridger Goodrich's arrival in 1777—along with the British troops—at last checked the open trade and the obvious sympathy with the mainland colonies.

Bridger Goodrich is a colorful figure. In spite of long connections with Bermuda and sympathy at first with the Patriots, he was converted to the royalist cause—strangely enough it seems—by Dunmore. He and his brothers arrived, soon to be followed by his father and by a group of Scotch-Irish adventurers, and together they transformed the island's role. He bought a large Bermuda-built sloop which had fallen a prize to the *Galataea* and, having refitted her as a privateer and renamed her the *Andrew Hammond,* after a naval captain whom he had known in Virginia, assumed command of her himself. Her trial run yielded five prizes in quick succession, two of them Bermudian vessels laden with Indian corn for the island, and Goodrich suggested that these be given up so that he could escape the odium of preying upon his neighbors. Nevertheless he made it clear that, except for authorized provision ships, he had no intention of letting Bermudian vessels go unmolested to the Continent. By the end of January 1778 he had taken nine prizes, seven Americans and two Bermudians. So long as he confined his privateering to American ships, the Bermudians looked on his enterprise with equanimity. He was in fact doing what the geographic position of the islands obviously suggested: in the Seven Years War, they had lived by just such privateering. Several other privateers were fitted out to cruise, more acceptably, against French and Spanish shipping as well as American; their success in capturing prizes increased the number of mouths to feed, however, and reduced Bermuda in 1780 to sore straits.

Goodrich was far from welcome. He was a brash newcomer, doing too well at the islands' expense, and imperilling their tortuous relations with the mainland. When the War was over, Colonel Henry Tucker, living in and enjoying London, reported that the Goodriches were doing the same, with a fortune estimated at £100,000. Later, they moved to Bristol—like many other Loyalists—and in the end Bridger Goodrich returned to Bermuda. But as early as 1778 local Bermuda leaders—Henry Tucker, John Harvey and George Bascome—had organised a "General Association" to boycott Goodrich's activities, and to hold no commercial dealings with privateers. When Captain Pender of the British privateer *Triumph* called at the west end of the island, he could get no supplies; when in 1780, however, on the advice of his Bermuda-born second-in-command, he hoisted the Stars and Stripes, 14 or 15 boats went out with supplies. In fact, Goodrich defeated the boycott, and by 1780, 91 prizes, many French, had passed through Admiralty Court. Goodrich did well indeed, and celebrated by marrying Elizabeth Tucker, the colonel's niece. A tax on privateers was imposed by the local assembly. When the Massachusetts Loyalist and former judge of the Boston Supreme Court, William Browne became Governor of Bermuda in 1782, replacing the vigorous Lieutenant-Governor George Bruere (G.J.'s eldest son) privateering was discouraged as likely to "draw the resentment of the enemy."[6]

Other Virginian Loyalists in Bermuda were less colorful figures. Dr. Archibald Campbell of Norfolk, one of Dunmore's partisans and a cousin of the Tuckers, did not leave Virginia until May 1776, when he sailed for Bermuda with his family in the sloop of war *Nautilus* under Captain John Collins. During the War his services were in demand, notably when smallpox struck. In 1784 he returned to Virginia to recover debts and remained there for five years in a vain effort to secure the passage of an act authorizing debt recovery. During his absence his family remained in Bermuda. He obtained from Governor William Browne a certificate testifying to his character and loyalty, and he appears later as Speaker of Assembly in the Bahamas.

Andrew Cazneau, the former Boston vice-admiralty judge, also spent some years in Bermuda after his banishment from Massachusetts. He became a councillor during his three-year stay, and in 1780 when Britain tried to take a stronger line with the Bermuda government he was appointed admiralty judge, obviously to tighten up the operation of the prize tribunals. He was supported by his fellow Bostonian Daniel Leonard ("Massachusettensis") who was moved from Barbados to become attorney-general alongside him. Scotsman Robert Traill was appointed collector of customs.

The Bermudian story for these years is a fascinating one. By 1782 the scale of the War against France and Spain permitted privateering not only to flourish but to become again legitimate. In the first four months of 1782 they captured no less than 34 prizes and by September a further 59. The people, wrote Traill, "now discover a spirit that fully convinces them they are at this period no friends to the Americans; for the fitting out of privateers in all ports of the islands in order to annoy their trade is becoming so general that there are now about eighteen sail commissioned and belonging to it.'' It was not quite unanimous. Some Bermudians (Thomas Roberts, Thomas Morgan, Ben Stiles and James Briggs) called on Washington in 1781 to invade the island, if necessary with French aid, promising popular support against British tyranny and suggesting a capitulation on similar terms to those accorded Grenada, giving neutrality while the war lasted. J.M. Varnum said that the task would require only 500 men and three or four frigates. Talk of invasion was in the air, but Britain's supremacy at sea by the summer of 1782 prevented any invasion.

George Bascome, lawyer-turned-merchant, summed up Bermuda's situation, though with only partial truth. Writing to St. George Tucker, 28th March 1778, he said,

> In the midsts of this mighty struggle for glory, dominion and liberty, poor little Bermuda has observed a strict neutrality. This perhaps you will say was the most difficult political manoeuvre that could be attempted. Be it so; God be thanked; the lives of 14,000 souls have been saved by it.

The recipient, himself strongly American in his sympathies, knew all too well the inaccuracy of this view. Yet if their role had been closer to that of ally than of neutral, and if the Tucker family were clearly Patriot at heart, it remains that to the majority of Bermudians the ties of loyalty did hold, cushioned after 1782 by the mounting evidence of the Royal Navy's presence and power. Needing American supplies, it had come close to disloyalty. It was held in line by the energy and courage of George Bruere, endlessly requesting more guns and more men, but never doubting ''the equity, honour and candour of government,'' and the unwelcome vigour of privateering Bridger Goodrich, who trusted no government and no neighbor.[7] Bruere died of wounds and exhaustion in 1785. Goodrich lived on in affluence. And so did the arch- compromiser Henry Tucker. Indeed by 1785 it was all as if it had been a tale for the chimney corner. Colonel Tucker returned from London to die in Bermuda in 1785. H.C. Wilkinson writes of it all in lyrical prose:

In the following spring the Colonel was restored to the embraces of his adoring household. He had written St. George in Virginia to send, or better to bring him, a good horse, and that dutiful son, undeterred by the events of the war, hastened to do so. He brought his family with him and spent three months at the homestead in Southampton. He rode that good horse over most of the island and was entertained everywhere, and his hospitable hosts, after clearing their dining-table and toasting the king, never failed to raise their glasses for the second time to the honour of General Washington. When the weeks were spent and St. George had to sail again to Virginia, he looked back upon his holiday as the happiest period of his life, but his father felt the parting had left a chasm in his heart. The Colonel lived until April 1785, and his last days were cheered by the progress which his second son, Thomas Tudor, was making in the 'metropolis' of New York. This son lived to be Treasurer of the United States. In view of that success, it is not strange that his elder brother in St. George's, the Honourable Henry, sometimes felt discouraged in his useful work, and increasingly lonely as his large family of boys left him one by one to enter the service of the Empire. But to the end the Colonel had recognized no favourite among his able and dutiful children, and left his estate to be equally divided among them, irrespective of their worldly positions or political beliefs.[8]

As Wilkinson also notes, Bermudians in fact lived at the center of an Imperial network, and in the next generation were to treat the mercantile world as peculiarly their own.

The enterprising members of the younger generation of Bermudians, however, were dubious about commerce coming to them and felt that it was their part to sally forth into the world. They went in all directions. Some of the sailors accepted Mediterranean passes to protect themselves against the Barbary pirates while on their voyages to the southern European ports. Simultaneously, a small flotilla of sloops went to Newfoundland to fish, but found, to their chagrin, that, by the terms of the recent Treaty, they were without rights in those waters and had no alternative but to return empty to their own island. In the meantime several lads with mercantile ability established themselves in some of the larger ports. Within a few years there were Tucker and Dickinson and also William Shedden in New York; Eliston and Perot in Philadelphia; Jennings and Wood as well as William Somersall at Charleston; Somersall and Son at St. Kitt's, where the head of that house was soon to become most friendly with Prince William Henry; Hodge and Forbes at St. Eustatius, and in due course Bermudian merchants were listed at St. John's, Newfoundland. At the same time, in other fields, Anthony George Forbes was making a most creditable start in medicine and in literature at Edinburgh, and Francis, the eldest son of Dr. Forbes, was starting upon a distinguished legal career which later took him to the antipodes. Henry St. George, the eldest son of the Honourable Henry Tucker, following his Bruere uncles, entered upon the service of the East India Company of which in time he was to become Auditor-General. Several of his brothers joined him in India. In the career of arms, meanwhile, another Forbes and two more of the Tucker boys became colonels in the Peninsular War under Wellington.

THE RESTORATION OF CIVIL GOVERNMENT BY THE BRITISH IN THE WAR OF INDEPENDENCE

BY

K.G. DAVIES

I

THE question of when and how to reestablish civil authority in the parts of North America held by the British did not fully emerge until after the failure of the Carlisle commission of 1778. At the beginning of the war neither the difficulties nor the potential advantages of restoring civil government were perceived. In New England the matter did not arise; well before the end of 1775 all British authority was defunct save at Boston, whither the civil officers who escaped capture had fled. Here, in circumstances of siege, civil power was completely eclipsed by the military. The Council of Massachusetts (nominated under the Act of Parliament of 1774) continued to meet at least until the end of October 1775, but Lieut.-Governor Thomas Oliver, presiding after Gates's departure, acknowledged that there was no place for civilian initiative: "The civil government here should be considered in a secondary view . . . I shall therefore be extremely cautious of any exercise of civil power which may in any degree tend to embarrass the service. . . ." In the months before the British quit Boston, the only business Oliver reported having transacted was the issue of letters of marque to armed vessels sailing to the West Indies.[1]

111

Elsewhere in the rebellious colonies British civil authority was equally dead but its revival appeared more practicable. What the American Department contemplated in 1775 was in the nature of a large-scale police operation, at the conclusion of which the ancient forms of civil government would be reestablished as a matter of course. A small number of ill-designing leaders of sedition would doubtless have to be punished, but since the majority of Americans outside New England were thought to be either loyal to the Crown or at worst 'deluded' no special difficulty was envisaged. This attitude is expressed in orders given on 6 December 1775 by Lord George Germain to the commander of the British southern expedition.[2] Circumstances appeared to favor an attempt "to effect the restoration of legal government." Reports from Georgia and the Carolinas promised support for the British cause; the governors and many of the civil officers of the colonies concerned were still on the spot and ready to resume their functions; the orders to Maj.-General Clinton admitted the existence of no political or legal problem. He was to begin by proclaiming pardon for all Americans who laid down their arms, with exceptions to be notified by the appropriate civil governor; anyone remaining in arms thereafter was to be arrested. Provincial Congresses and Committees were to be dissolved and the civil courts immediately reopened. Apparently no act of state was deemed necessary to reestablish royal government; it would just happen when the police operation was complete.

Possibly the signing of these orders started doubts in the American Department whether the *status quo ante bellum* could be restored by so simple a device as the letter of one of the Principal Secretaries of State. Three days later Germain instructed the Crown's law officers to prepare a commission for restoring peace in America, granting pardons to rebels, and inquiring into the state of the colonies.[3] The product in due course was the first of the peace-commissions, that to the Howe brothers, issued on 6 May 1776. The instructions accompanying the commission defined the political concessions Britain was willing to make, not large enough to tempt Congress, but quite important by pre-war standards and evidence of at least an elementary British understanding that the war might be influenced by political action.[4] With regard to the restoration of civil government, the commissioners were empowered to declare "any colony or province, or any county, town, port, district or place within the said colonies" to be at the King's peace provided certain conditions were met. Congresses and Committees must be dissolved and "constitutional officers of government allowed to resume their functions." Bodies of armed men must be disbanded, and there must be fair prospects of compensation for loss of property. Any colony where these conditions were fulfilled, and where an Assembly met, declared its allegiance to the King and applied for relief from the Prohibitory Act, qualified to be "at peace." It is clear from these instructions that the revival of civil government was viewed at this time, not as a tactical move to attract American support, but as something incidental to the formal purging of rebellion.

A weakness of the Howe commission was the uncertainty how negotiations with the Americans were meant to be conducted. The commissioners thought themselves authorized to negotiate with representatives of Congress, and did so at the Staten Island meeting on 11 September 1776; when nothing came of that, all the Howes could think of was an appeal to the people at large by circulating a printed declaration and inviting professions of loyalty.[5] The idea of creating alternative American governments, wherever practicable, and negotiating with them, seems not to have occurred to the commissioners. Another weakness, and perhaps more serious, was that authority to restore America or any part of it to the King's peace was bestowed exclusively upon the commanders-in-chief of the army and navy, as it was in every subsequent peace-commission sent across the Atlantic, except that of 1778. Germain, reflecting upon these expedients near the end of his public career, laid it down that "the finishing of the war should not so absolutely depend upon the decision of those whose interest in continuing it may in some degree influence their judgments."[6] The innuendo is probably unfair to the Howes and certainly unfair to Clinton; but it is unfair to none of the British commanders to suggest that they were apprehensive of the restraints a civil power could lay upon military freedom of action. They feared civilian interference, not because it might put an end to the war and their own importance, but because it was likely to restrain or divert their military operations. The disagreements that sprang up in later years were not between those

who wanted to prolong the fighting and those who wanted to end
it, but between exponents of different conceptions of how the war
might be won.

Nowhere in the proceedings of the Howe commission is there
recognition of the possibility of using restored civil government as a
political weapon to advance the British cause and discomfort the
rebels. Confirmation of this negative attitude comes from the
refusal of the commissioners to contemplate restoring civil government in the only place where in 1776 it was practicable to do so, the
part of New York recovered by the British army. The Howes took
the view that the area was too small and that it would be "inexpe-
dient" to open the port to trade or privateering, by which they
meant that warlike stores would be smuggled through British territory to the rebels and that there would be fewer seamen available
for impressment. Germain, no more alive at this time than the
Howes to the potential advantage of restoring civil government,
agreed.[7] All the same, there would probably have been at least
debate on the expediency of reviving civil authority in New York in
1776 but for Governor Tryon's ambition for military command,
which removed the pressure for restoring civil government to be expected from those who got a living by it. Tryon sided with the
Howes when he wrote a few days after the capture of the city:

> As this country is in the present period too much con-
> vulsed for the civil government to act with any good ef-
> fect, it is the opinion of both His Majesty's commis-
> sioners for restoring peace to the colonies that I should
> postpone any executive acts of government until the
> province is more liberated from the control of the
> rebels. I therefore have kept the executive powers of
> civil government dormant, leaving everything to the
> direction of the military[8]

There it remained throughout 1777. The boundaries of British-held
New York contracted rather than expanded. Tryon, now major-
general of provincials, was hardly able, as he put it, "to sit within
the shade of my government."[9] The port of New York remained
virtually closed, to the chagrin of Britons like Samuel Martin of

Whitehaven who claimed to be bleeding at every pore from neglect of the city's commercial interests.[10] Instead of a beacon of prosperity and constitutional freedom beckoning to American victims of inflation and the draft, New York in 1777 was a military camp.

On a broader view, the state of civil affairs in British-held America was by no means helpful to the British claim to be fighting for the restoration of constitutional liberty against the oligarchical tyranny of Congresses and Committees. Civil government survived in all six colonies which still acknowledged King George III in the sense that the courts stayed open and trade with Britain, subject to restrictions, was permitted. But in three of these colonies— Newfoundland, Quebec, East Florida—no representative Assembly had ever been constituted; in a fourth, West Florida, the Assembly had last met in 1772 and been dissolved following conflict with the governor; while in the Island of St. John (Prince Edward Island) the House of Representatives that had struggled into existence in 1773 lapsed soon after the outbreak of war. In all British North America only one representative body—the Assembly of Nova Scotia—met and passed laws in 1777.

II

Defeat at Saratoga and the imminent entry of France into the war stimulated new thinking and a greater awareness of the need for political initiative. The fruit of this awareness was the Carlisle commission of 12 April 1778. For the first and only time civilians were put into a peace-commission; not only that, they outnumbered the military by three (Carlisle, Eden, Johnstone) to two and, when Lord Howe declined to serve, the majority became three to one (Clinton). This time the commissioners were expressly authorized to negotiate with Congress; indeed they were told to negotiate with no one else, for fear of giving umbrage, until they were certain that the approach to Congress had failed. Then came the concessions, contained or at least contemplated in the instructions accompanying the commission.[11] They need not be rehearsed here; sufficient to say that they included everything a colonial heart could desire. The only matters declared non-negotiable were independence and the payment by Britain of America's war expenditure. All that Britain asked in return was a voluntary contribution to the common defence fund, restitution of property and reversal of forfeitures, and the restoration of the Church of England clergy. Given that Britain intended to continue as an imperial power in America, no more generous offer—nor any more attractively packaged—could have been made.

The commissioners went first to Philadelphia, then to New York which they reached on 29 June 1778; by 7 July they knew that their approach to Congress had failed. On that day they wrote to Germain that nothing could be expected "except through the exertion of His Majesty's arms or by an appeal to the people at large or by negotiations with separate bodies of men and individuals."[12] Later the commissioners became convinced that even the concession of independence would not buy a treaty with the rulers of America; Congress had pledged itself to France and hoped before peace was made to win Bermuda and the rest of the continent while the French picked up Newfoundland and some of the British sugar-colonies.[13] It was out of this total wreck of the Carlisle negotiations that the plan was born for reestablishing civil government as a means of influencing opinion against Congress and of convincing Americans of British sincerity. For, despite their failure, the commissioners believed that leverage existed and that Americans, if not their rulers, could be moved. What this leverage was they explained in a secret letter of 16 November 1778: the distresses of war, the depreciation of the currency, the harshness of the new governments, and the unpopularity of the French alliance. On these foundations an alternative to rebel authority might be built if, but only if, British promises to restore liberty and rights of property could be made to appear credible. To try the "experiment" the commissioners resolved to empower Lieut.-Colonel Archibald Campbell, then on the point of sailing to Savannah with 3500 men, to transform a military operation into a political initiative.

> The plan to which we allude implies such an application of His Majesty's force on this continent as may protect the pacific and well-affected subjects of His Majesty in

resuming the civil government that is offered to them and put them in a condition to defend their persons and their properties and to turn against the enemies of peace the ed e of criminal law, under the pretence of which many o. the well-affected subjects of the King are at present made cruelly to suffer.

We wished to have it clearly understood that military force was not to be employed in this country but with an ultimate purpose of enabling His Majesty's faithful subjects to resume their civil governments with such redress of grievances, whether real or supposed, and with such farther security for rights as His Majesty in Parliament had been and might be pleased to grant. And upon this idea we thought it might conduce to the success of the service on which Lieutenant-Colonel Campbell was employed that he should be received in the discharge of his military duty as a person disposed and qualified to restore the civil government of the province in case the inhabitants were inclined to accept of his protection for that purpose.[14]

Campbell was given commissions as civil governor of Georgia and, in case his operations should extend so far, of South Carolina as well.[15] His success was beyond expectation. Having taken Savannah on 29 December 1778, he proclaimed the intention of restoring civil government on 4 January and set up an interim Board of Police to aid the military. Before this Board could get to grips with the civil problems of Georgia, it was dissolved on 4 March and the restoration of civil government declared. Shortly afterwards Campbell sailed for England, leaving Lieut.-Colonel John Mark Prevost in charge as lieut.-governor.

All this had come about with remarkable speed. The Carlisle commissioners in trying their "experiment" had not exceeded their powers (which included the appointment of civil governors) but they seem to have acted on their own initiative; certainly they acted without direct orders from home. Germain, though not best pleased with their general conduct, nevertheless reacted favorably to the initiative. It is indeed clear from a letter of his which crossed with the commissioners' secret dispatch of 16 November that he had already begun to think on the same lines: reestablished civil government, he wrote, might serve as "an example . . . of the advantages to be enjoyed by those who submit . . ."[16] When the commissioners returned home and reported to the Cabinet, Germain was filled with enthusiasm. As early as 23 January, well before the outcome of the Georgia expedition was known, he encouraged Clinton to drive back Washington's army so as to remove the "chief objection to the reestablishment of civil government in New York . . ." and to dispel American fears "of being ruled by military laws in all time to come. . . ."[17] This phrase, or something like it, occurs in other letters emanating from the American Department at this time. On 31 March Sir James Wright was ordered to return to Georgia and summon an Assembly as soon as possible so that "the inhabitants of all the provinces may see it is not the intention of His Majesty in Parliament to govern America by military law, but on the contrary to allow them all the benefits of a local legislature and their former civil constitution."[18] The need to allay American apprehensions was again expressed in a letter to Tryon on 1 April announcing Maj.-General James Robertson's appointment as the new civil governor of New York; and Robertson's orders of 9 July were drafted in practically the same terms as those respecting Georgia given to Wright.[19] Meanwhile Clinton was assured that the Georgia experiment was working and that the people of South Carolina were likely to want the same benefits: "The restoring Georgia to peace and the reestablishment of civil government there will I hope serve to increase that disposition and induce them to invite instead of opposing the introduction of the King's troops there."[20] By 5 August, racing ahead of the result of the Georgia experiment, Germain was convinced that "our utmost efforts will fail of their effect if we cannot find means to engage the people of America in support of a cause which is equally their own and ours. . . ."[21]

III

Germain's instructions to Governor Wright of 31 May 1779 show that restored royalist Georgia was intended to be different from the America envisaged in the Carlisle commissioners' instructions.[22] The immediate danger seemed now to be over; gone were the ultra-generous concessions put forward to dish the French. If the British were going to fight instead of negotiate their way to peace, they meant to recover at least part of their pre-war imperial status. The old Council of Georgia was dissolved by royal fiat and the governor authorized to nominate twelve new members, among them none "who have not given full assurance of their loyalty and attachment to the constitution. . . ." The Assembly was to be summoned as soon as possible and given three tasks: nullification of all proceedings since the rebellion; the arming of the executive with powers to check rebellion in the future; and the settlement of claims for injuries and losses caused to loyal subjects. The matter of the contribution to the general charge of empire was approached more circumspectly: "Should Georgia take the lead in so dutiful and grateful a measure, it could not fail of recommending the province to peculiar favour and obtaining for her some extraordinary indulgence." More tangibly a *quid pro quo* was offered in the form of remission of arrears of quitrents and an undertaking that they and the colony's casual revenues would in future be applied to services within Georgia. Further changes were not ruled out "tending more firmly to unite the province with Great Britain and to render that union indissoluble."

When Wright landed at Savannah on 14 July 1779 he had in his pocket an instrument drawn up in London by the Carlisle commissioners for restoring Georgia to the King's peace, to use or not at his discretion.[23] His first shock was to find his thunder stolen by Campbell's establishment of civil government four months previously, notice of which had not reached Whitehall when he sailed. Somewhat plaintively he reported that the Prohibitory Act, which he should have had the credit for suspending, was "totally disregarded and set aside."[24] His second shock was the discovery that Georgia was by no means as reduced to order as he had supposed. As well as the newly-ceded territories, Augusta and the lands thereabout down to Briar Creek were in the hands of rebels whose raiding parties reached to within twenty miles of the Savannah. Without the army's presence there was real danger of the province being totally lost.[25] Wright's third shock came on 8

September when there appeared off Tybee twenty-five French ships of the line, nine frigates, and an army of four to five thousand men presently joined by fifteen hundred Americans.

In fact the French assault turned out to be a blessing in disguise; it was beaten off with heavy loss and the prospects of breathing life into Georgia's restored civil institutions much improved. Wright, however, still hesitated to take the decisive step of summoning an Assembly.[26] Germain repeatedly ordered him to do so but it was not until after Clinton and his army had arrived in the south in January 1780 that he steeled himself to issue the writs. The hesitation is understandable. Probably most of Georgia's "notorious rebels" had betaken themselves to South Carolina but, until an Assembly had met and enacted statutory disqualifications, all who had been eligible under the old constitution to vote and to be elected were eligible to do so in 1780. Wright was afraid of meeting a carbon-copy of the Assemblies he had faced before the war. Elections were finally held in April in every parish except one (St Paul's) and the Assembly met on 9 May, three days before Charleston surrendered to Clintn.[27] It sat for most of the summer, was recalled in the autumn to deal with the problem of guerillas, and met again in 1781. On the whole it behaved better than expected. Despite Wright's complaint letter in 1780 that too many members who "savoured of the old leaven" had crept in at by-elections, the Assembly got through a remarkable amount of work in its fifteen months of life, most of it to Whitehall's satisfaction.[28] It voted an address of congratulation to the governor and one of loyalty to the King. Thirty-three Acts were passed, at least one of which contained the suspending clause—till the King's pleasure be known—to which American Assemblies had so much objected in former years. A Disqualifying Act, without running to excess, modified over-generous concessions of pardon; 146 named persons were barred from sitting in the Assembly or holding offices of trust. In 1781 the Assembly passed an Act of Attainder against twenty-three named rebels and, best of all, it voted a duty of 2½ per cent on the colony's exports as Georgia's contribution to the general charges of the British empire. Five per cent was proposed but thought excessive in the prevailing poverty; as Wright said, it was the principle that mattered, the sum could probably be raised later on. A legislative program like this would have been regarded as astonishingly successful in the 1760s or 1770s, and gratifying at any time in colonial historty. Whatever else put an end to British government in Georgia, it was not the deadlock between governor and Assembly that had bedevilled pre-war politics in nearly every American colony.[29]

Harmony in the legislature did not necessarily translate into effective executive action. Georgia's pre-war government had been weak and impoverished; its restored government was far from strong, still poor despite Parliamentary aid, and now faced with problems of far greater difficulty. Wright's chief failure on the civil front was in meeting the demand of loyalists for reparations. In London the measure doubtless looked practicable as well as just: estates belonging to unpardoned rebels should be confiscated and handed over to those who had suffered. On the spot the problem was more complicated. Considerable confusion existed as to who had and who had not been pardoned. Wright believed that under Clinton's proclamation of 3 March 1780 pardon was available to everyone who returned to obedience; he did not realize that the restoration of civil government in Georgia had removed his province from the orbit of the commissioner for restoring peace. Until the end of 1780 there seemed to be nothing to stop even "notorious rebels" from submitting for the sake of preserving their estates and continuing covertly to support the rebel cause; such was "the nest of Oliverians" in St John's parish who had distressed Wright in former years and now returned to haunt him. Even where rebels were absent from the colony, their estates were anything but easy meat for hungry loyalists; they might be burdened with debts owing to persons whose conduct did not merit forfeiture; to seize such properties would be to gratify one set of friends at the expense of another. Worst of all was the hard fact of economic life: a deserted estate, stripped of its stock and slaves, was worth next to nothing in the circumstances of 1780-81. "I don't see," the governor wrote, "that there is anything at all to be had or expected . . . I am really at a loss to know what the Assembly can do to put it in my power to make any compensation to the loyal refugees for their losses."[30]

It might have been possible to live with less than fully satisfied loyalists; what impaired civil government in Georgia from the beginning was a military problem it could neither solve nor live with. The menace of the rebel partisans in the neighborhood of Augusta rose and fell according to the fortunes of British arms in South Carolina but it never vanished. Many of the sixty letters written by Wright to Germain from his landing in the colony to the coming of the news of Yorktown reported murders and plundering committed on loyal inhabitants, often far down the river towards Savannah. Not that the partisans were formidable in number: no more than five hundred, Wright told Clinton in February 1780.[31] But they were enough to undermine the experiment of setting up a civil government which was meant to be responsible for its own defence. The intention had been, and remained, that those who had been delivered from tyranny would secure their own liberties "without calling for the aid of any considerable number of His Majesty's troops. . . ."[32] Wright, apt to forget this part of the bargain, pleaded for a force of 800 foot and 150 horse, "and with this force I think rebellion cannot rear its head again in Georgia . . ." but he pleaded in vain.[33]

Georgia's inability to defend itself from the partisans does not necessarily denote unwillingness on the part of loyalists to help themselves. Though in some ways ideal for the experiment of restored government, Georgia was neither rich nor populous enough in 1779-81 to assume the whole burden of its own defence. "I have ordered an exact return of the whole military. . . ." the governor wrote soon after he arrived. "I really believe they will not exceed 400 men in the whole province and probably 300 would not appear under arms."[34] Money was the trouble. Wright had to argue hard to get even rations for the Georgia militia; pay, Germain positively refused for fear of setting a precedent. "How is it to be expected," Wright asked, "or indeed possible for a poor man who has a family who in a great measure depend on his daily labour to leave that family to starve while he goes out on duty and how is he to subsist even himself?"[35] Precluded by the nature of the political experiment from adopting the harsh measures Americans used to comb out the militia, Wright could do little but beg. In March 1781 a small troop of horse was formed—sixty-nine officers and men— paid out of the £5000 Parliament had granted to Georgia, but by then Cornwallis's advance into North Carolina and his involvement with Greene had put the partisans of the western frontier into a state of comparative safety. Wright's letters thenceforward tell of royal Georgia's sinking condition.

IV

South Carolina, with stronger anti-colonial traditions, set British policy and British sincerity a more searching test than Georgia, at the same time offering a greater prize. If Charleston's trade with Britain could be reopened, and civil government restored, evidence would indeed be forthcoming of the benefits of submission to the Crown. At the moment Charleston fell (12 May 1780), the intention to return South Carolina to its pre-war condition undoubtedly prevailed on the British side; Germain expected it, so did the civil officers of the colony on the spot or waiting in England to be called back, so did the British merchants trading to South Carolina, so did some if not all of the British military and naval commanders. But the experiment was not tried, the courts remained closed, the Assembly never met. What went wrong?

The short answer is that the British never pacified the colony to a point where civil government could be reinstated with a guarantee of success. The "golden dreams" engendered by the taking of Charleston were quickly dispersed. Camden, one of the most brilliant victories of the whole war, soon took its place in the line of British triumphs bearing little or no fruit.[36] South of the Saluda and Santee Rivers the British contrived a position in the summer of 1780 that was reasonably secure; north was a battleground.[37] The question cannot, however, be answered in exclusively military terms. The restoration of civil government in an area still affected by war must always be fraught with risk; the policy had, after all, been devised as a tactic to aid the army's progress, not as a garland to crown the successful ending of a campaign. Despite the fragility of Cornwallis's situation, there were many on the British side in 1780 and at the beginning of 1781 who thought that the experiment should be tried.

The most persuasive advocate of civil government for South Carolina was James Simpson, the colony's attorney-general, secretary of the commander-in-chief's council, and Clinton's political adviser on South Carolina matters. He entered Charleston with the British troops and reported to Clinton on civil affairs three days after the capitulation.[38] "It will," he wrote, "be very practicable to reestablish the King's government in South Carolina although it will require both time and address." Too much dependence, he thought, should not be placed on the loyalists: they were fewer than he had expected and already a bit of a nuisance with their clamor for "retributive justice." The rest of the people he divided into four categories: those who had supported rebellion but were now convinced of their mistake; those, never deeply committed, who feared that ruin would ensue if the rebellion went on; those who still thought the American cause "founded in virtue" but deemed it impossible to continue the fight; and those who said "it ought never to be relinquished but with the general consent of America." "Conviction operates upon those I first mentioned, interest upon the second, and despair upon the third . . ." The fourth category he thought was outnumbered by the others. As for the lower class, "they will without trouble submit quietly to the government that supports itself."

This report may be deemed optimistic but it was not absurd. In the nine months Simpson spent in South Carolina he enjoyed some successes. Prominent among them was the reopening of trade between Charleston and Britain in August and September 1780 when ten ships sailed under convoy with cargoes worth, Simpson was informed, more than £100,000.[39] This was the way to win the Carolinians as well as to please the merchants at home. With tobacco coming more than two hundred miles to catch the convoy, the prospect was opened of diffusing prosperity to the distant parts of the province. Nor was this all. Simpson worked hard in his office of intendant-general of the Board of Police, which met for the first time on 13 June 1780 to "advise and assist" the military. Under his guidance measures were adopted which, while not restoring civil institutions to their former vigour, tended to soften the blatancy of a military regime. Thus on 1 August the Board proposed and the military agreed that fit persons should be appointed justices of the peace for Charleston. Wherever possible, in its varied administrative work, the Board acted in conformity with old laws. So, on 7 July, when considering the public health of Charleston, the Board resolved that "it would conduce greatly thereto if the Act for that purpose passed the 10th day of August 1764 was carried into execution." In similar spirit colonial Acts laying taxes on ships and goods imported by transients were revived and enforced in order to raise a fund for relieving Charleston's poor. In its judicial business, also, the Board used ancient practices, particularly those prescribed by the circuit court law, "always a great favourite with the people," which gave summary jurisdiction in all causes under £20 sterling.[40] Another step in the same direction was taken in February 1781 when Lieut.-Governor Bull and other civil officers at last arrived from England. Bull took over from Simpson as intendant-general Egerton Leigh joined the Board and at his death was succeeded by Thomas Knox Gordon, chief justice of the colony. Germain, while never ceasing to press for an early restoration of full civil government, took a hopeful view of these developments: "As it must be pleasing to the loyal inhabitants to see their former civil magistrates in the exercise of the powers under which they are governed, though the mode may be different, so may it lead the republican party to relish the rule of officers not of their own constituting and prepare them to pay obedience to royal authority.[41] Official British policy in 1781 continued to aim at convincing not just the people of South Carolina but all Americans that "no abridgement of their former liberties is intended. . . ."

The South Carolina Board of Police was frequently criticised by British civilians as a poor substitute for the real thing, as indeed it was. Simpson himself thought it "upon too narrow a scale to do ample justice" and regretted opportunities for calling the Assembly that had been allowed to slip away.[42] Egerton Leigh could find little good to say of the Board and wanted civil government fully restored the moment he arrived in the colony, "a sentiment which I suspect ill corresponds with military ideas."[43] Bull was more cautious but expressed the hope of seeing an Assembly soon in session. Despite these reservations, it would be wrong to dismiss the Board as merely a British confidence trick, a thin disguise for military rule, deceiving no one. Plenty of South Carolinians were ready to bring their civil causes to the Board, a hundred a month according to Simpson, and the surviving records bear him out.[44] More convincing is the number of persons who applied to the

Board for restoration to the status of British subject, a total between 17 June 1780 and 31 July 1781 of 1866 persons. Among those
who applied and were approved appear the names of Henry Mid-
dleton, second president of the Continental Congress, Rawlins
Lowndes, former president of South Carolina, and Charles Pinck-
ney, father of the future governor of the state: "and I have pretty
good information," Simpson added, "that several who are now at
Philadelphia are setting their faces this way for that purpose."[45] If
the British could make an impression on Americans like these, why
not on others?

One reason for the failure of British tentatives to mature into
full-scale restoration of civil government in South Carolina was
that the problems left behind by war were too complex and too
grave to be quickly resolved either by military authority or by colonial institutions of restricted resource. Simpson acknowledged
this. A difficulty he soon encountered was the large investments
made by South Carolinians in what he called "the American
funds." By 30 August 1780 he had discovered that "very many
people have been so credulous and infatuated as to place large sums
of money in their state treasury, some as far as one hundred thousand pounds sterling, and the loss of so much property by so many
persons cannot fail to have powerful effects.[46] Some of this money
had come from trust-funds, opening a prospect of endless litigation
should the civil courts be opened. Even more serious was the problem of inflation since 1775 and the trail of legal contracts made in
the then current money of the country. "There are some who insist
. . ." Simpson reported, "that the money should be estimated at
the proportioned values it formerly bore to gold and silver, whilst
the debtors insist that the money which was current at the time of
the contract though now of no value ought still to be received
. . ."[47] Such things were beyond the competence of the Board of
Police which, in general, confined itself to matters arising since the
taking of Charleston. Simpson, however, made a brave attempt to
tackle the problems of inflation by setting a committee to work
establishing a tariff of depreciation of South Carolina's currency,
which he hoped might be voluntarily accepted by disputants or better still enforced by law.[48]

Simpson left Charleston in February 1781, from which time the military situation deteriorated fairly steadily. That British South Carolina was sinking was plain well before Yorktown, for example in Lieut.-Governor Bull's report of 28 June 1781 of a prospect "too unpleasing to be enlarged on."[49] Simpson, back in New York, professed not to be surprised at this turn of events. With his liking for categories, he divided the enemy in South Carolina into four parts. First were the inveterates who could never be won over, only cowed. Secondly, there were the victims of loyalist excesses which the Board of Police was powerless to restrain. People in remote parts of the country "proceeded to do themselves justice, and by their violence drove out of the settlements many who would otherwise have peaceably remained at home and been useful in settling the quiet of the country." Thirdly, there were the prisoners taken by the British at Charleston who had escaped when the prisons were blown up in the explosion of 13 May 1780; Simpson put their number at one thousand. Finally, there were the "banditti" of the western frontier to whom all government was and ever had been obnoxious: "Having assumed the name of a party they conceive that they will not be amenable to the laws for their crimes." Even now Simpson did not give up his advocacy of civil government. In letters of 28 July and 20 August 1781 he admitted that British propaganda had not so far succeeded. The "tyrants," i.e. Congress, had proved strong enough to stamp out revolts engendered by their own oppression. The leverage, assumed to exist by the Carlisle commissioners three years earlier, had been shown to be insufficient. A greater inducement to peace was needed to overcome "a very general opinion that the government and constitution of the rebellious provinces have been so utterly subverted that they are absolutely extinct and cannot exist to any purpose."[50] Despair was what the British had to combat "by setting before them the example of felicity enjoyed by one of the provinces in consequence of a renewed amity with the parent state. Carolina in my humble opinion is a country in which the experiment may be tried with every probability of success . . . My plan is simply to convene the legislature." No other way was open; legal government was "the surest and indeed the only means to reconcile the people." Simpson closed his last letter with a comment worth taking seriously: "It is from their civil institutions that the rebels derive the whole of their strength, for in all the places which have been occupied by troops, whether they are British or American, disaffection to the cause in which they are engaged hath uniformly increased amongst the people. . . ."[51] In other words, the way for either side to win the war was to get its army out of sight at the earliest possible moment and to bring on its civil government. The British never felt confident enough to do this in South Carolina; it is possible to think that their cause declined through lack of belief in their own propaganda.

V

Restoration of civil government in North Carolina and Virginia was mentioned as a desirable eventuality should Cornwallis's northward advance have the success expected from it; it was proposed by Governor Franklin for New Jersey as a worthy strategic objective; and it was suggested by Charles Dudley, a former Customs officer, for Rhode Island.[52] In none of these colonies did the matter become practical politics. The only place, apart from Georgia and South Carolina, where the British had the opportunity to revive civil government was New York. Here, as we have already seen, a chance had been lost in 1776. No step towards restoring normal life was taken until 26 September 1778 when the Carlisle commissioners opened the ports of New York and Newport, R.I., subject to restrictions intended to meet the navy's objections; the resulting activities in trade, disposal of accumulated prize-goods, and privateering, appear to have been regarded as more beneficial than harmful.[53] With the Georgia experiment in full swing in 1779, Germain was enthusiastic to see the strategy of restored civil government extended to New York. Hence the appointment of Robertson to succeed Tryon, and hence Robertson's orders of 9 July to summon an Assembly and to proceed on the lines laid down for Governor Wright in Georgia. There was, however, an important difference between the arrangements for Georgia and the arrangements for New York. In the former case a decision had already been made by the Carlisle commissioners to restore the colony to the King's peace; the matter was out of the commander-in-chief's hands. In the latter case that decision had not been taken; the Carlisle commission on 31 May 1779 expired and Clinton was, or was about to be made, sole commissioner in America. Robertson's orders, therefore, were necessarily conditional upon Clinton's approval. Germain hoped that this approval would be forthcoming, "in which case the civil constitution will revive and your authority as civil governor become competent. . . ."[54]

Robertson did not reach New York until 21 March 1780; Clinton was in the south, so that the question of giving effect to Germain's orders did not immediately arise. When Clinton returned in mid-June Robertson found himself involved in a major row between the two commanders-in-chief, now joint commissioners for restoring peace. Clinton and Arbuthnot had disagreed over restoring civil government to South Carolina; now they transferred the venue of dispute to New York. Robertson put the best face on affairs when he wrote on 1 July:

> As the General and the Admiral have acquainted your lordship of their different sentiments about the renewal of civil government, they and the state will benefit by the appeal; but [as] no advantage could arise from the public or even the Council's being informed that they did not think alike on the subject, I have taken some pains to keep the question out of sight. And as these gentlemen equally intend that the subject be protected in his property, be secured against the abuses and insults of military misrule, that a good police and good discipline may make the neighbourhood of the army advantageous to the inhabitants, and the industry of these, being excited by security and order, useful to the state, Sir Henry means to direct me to take the management of the police of the province, and subject to his inspection to endeavour to give the people all the encouragement and real advantages graciously intended them by His Majesty on my appointment. The Admiral expresses his approbation of the expedient. For my part I shall most gladly exert my utmost endeavours to answer the end of my appointment. If I can serve His Majesty and have the honour of executing the spirit of the instructions you honoued me with, I care no more than the people will by what name I am called.[55]

Clinton's concessions were minor gestures, unlikely to convince his own side of the benevolence of British intentions, let alone the enemy. Civilian magistrates or arbitrators were appointed to act summarily and without fee in the portion of New York held by the British, and Ludlow, formerly a judge, was made superintendent for Long Island, an office Clinton considered military and which was paid for out of the military fund.[56] Robertson, despite formal acquiescence, was not satisfied with these tokens. "I think," he wrote on 28 January 1781, "that a loyal American Assembly might at this time hold to Americans a language useful to Britain, and I know that from the places within our protection we could call more than half the number of representatives that usually formed the Assembly."[57] Clinton remained unpersuaded. On the question of reviving the collection of duties by Customs officers at the port of New York—no local affair but something ordered by the British Treasury—he defined his position: "whilst this city continues under military government no interference of civil officers can be allowed. . . ."[58] There the matter rested to the end of 1781. New York was not declared at the King's peace and no further progress was made towards a revival of civil institutions, with consequences held by Chief Justice William Smith to be "very mischievous to the interests of Great Britain. . . ."[59]

Clinton's attitude towards civil government needs careful definition. He himself claimed to be "as much for civil government as any man . . . as soon as it consisted with the general good . . ." but it is as the arch-opponent of civil authority that he appears in relation to the experiments of 1779 and 1780.[60] True, he was party to the original plan to revive civil government in Georgia but he soon regretted it. Governor Wright, held to the contract that a restored government should provide for its own defence, came to suspect that the military did not wish well to the Georgia experiment. He wrote to Knox of the American Department:

> The Generals &c have always Set their faces against this Province, as I have frequently Wrote you, and I can't tell why, unless it is because the King has thought Proper to re-establish his Civil Government here— which the Military cannot bear—and I have long seen

they will do Nothing for us, without a Positive order from Home & which may now be too late.[61]

South Carolina was the scene of the difference of opinion (or perhaps the clash of temperament expressed as a difference of opinion) between Clinton and Arbuthnot, the military and naval commanders-in-chief and, from April 1780, joint commissioners for restoring peace. Arbuthnot wanted to punish the obnoxious in South Carolina, disarm the rest, and "establish the British Constitution in its fullest extent immediately as an example for the sister colony to embrace."[62] Clinton acknowledged that restoration must come but wanted it to come gradually:

> The violent commotions that have prevailed will not admit of the instant return of that regular and gentle flow by which formerly justice was distributed and government conducted. The interposition of the magistrate in criminal matters may conduce very much to establish the peace and quiet of the country when to open the courts of civil law would increase confusion and be productive of many other bad consequences.[63]

This is to put a generous construction on his own resistance to civil government. There is another side, shown in New York: his determination that the army should never be hindered or embarrassed by the interference of civilians. There is reason to think that he was ready to resign rather than see New York's "civil rights" restored.[64] Viewed in this light, South Carolina and New York were different prospects. After the fall of Charleston, Clinton could look forward to a time when Cornwallis would pass beyond the colony's border, leaving a pacified country behind him; then civil government could take over. No such hope could be entertained for New York; until it could, civil government was to be resisted. Clinton's attitude was a practical one, even a sensible one, but it was unsympathetic to the original purpose of reviving civil government. The Carlisle commissioners, and Germain, intended to wage political warfare, to use the King's peace and restored civil authority to prise open Congress's grip on America. Such a policy involved risks and inconvenience but the rewards of success would have been great; Clinton saw only the risks and the inconvenience.

VI

There are two unexpected and somewhat perplexing postscripts to the British design to restore civil government in America and Clinton's attitude towards it. The first came in August 1781 at the moment when Cornwallis was locking himself into Yorktown. After resisting civil government for South Carolina when it might possibly have had useful consequences, Clinton suddenly reversed his thinking and declared to Simpson his readiness to endorse a "fit plan" provided Cornwallis approved and provided it did not "devigorate military operations. . . ."[65] It was not his intention to put the colony formally at the King's peace but he promised all the support for civil institutions he could give as commander-in-chief and as commissioner. Simpson thought the moment had come at last and began to devise ways of reconciling civil and military authority; but before the matter could be taken further, Cornwallis's surrender removed it from the realm of practical politics.

The second postscript is even odder. On 23 January 1782, after years of standing in the path of civil government in New York, Clinton announced that he had withdrawn his opposition and was passing the decision over to Governor Robertson.[66] No sufficient explanation for this *renversement* was supplied in Clinton's brief report to Germain (also signed by Robert Digby, joint commissioner), only a hint that it might be necessary "to enable us to meet the rebels on the ground taken up by General Washington in his answer to the 10th article of the capitulation of York Town."[67] Some on the British side, Clinton presumably among them, believed that the article put loyalist troops at risk; William Franklin thought it placed them "in no better light than as runaway slaves restored to their former masters," and pressed Clinton to make a public declaration that loyalist troops would never be surrendered on different terms from the King's troops.[68] Others wanted a threat of retaliation. Clinton was at first agreeable, later decided it would not be expedient for the military to act in this way, and hit upon the notion of opening the civil courts of New York as a means "to quiet the minds of loyalists. . . ." Just how this would allay these particular apprehensions of the loyalists he did not explain. Robertson, reporting the business, scarcely troubled to hide his amazement. Everyone he consulted expressed "a surprise that, after a measure had been so long suppressed while it might have been of service to the King, it should be proposed under circumstances similar to those which induce other governors to declare military law."[69] Robertson's own opinion was that now was not the moment for what he had long wished to see; the Council of New York concurred.[70] Possibly Clinton was practising a *politique du pire,* making the worst of a bad job, and creating maximum embarrassment for his subordinates and successor. Or perhaps one should not expect rational and consistent conduct, especially in the last days of his command, from a commander-in-chief who had suffered so much and so long.

THE CLAIMS:
THE MISSION OF JOHN ANSTEY

BY

L. F. S. UPTON

═══════════════════

The commissioners meeting at Lincoln's Inn Fields to enquire into the losses and services of the American Loyalists had early become aware of the difficulty of evaluating the testimony of claimants before them. Their first report lamented that there was no way to communicate with "proper Persons in the different States" to obtain copies of records of confiscation and sequestration, of title deeds and encumbrances on title. The claimants could not be expected to have brought complete documentary proofs with them in their exile, and yet the onus was on them to contact the various registrars and authorities on the other side of the Atlantic to get such proofs. Having left their homeland under a cloud the claimants now found it difficult to get copies and the commissioners were being forced to rely on the oath of the claimants and other witnesses for assertions that cried aloud for documentary support: oaths, the commissioners austerely concluded, were "too slender a security uniformly to be relied on." When the 1783 act establishing the Loyalist Commission was renewed in 1785 it included a clause authorising the appointment of a proper person to resort to the United States to gather information "for better ascertaining the several claims" presented before the Commission.[1] That proper person was John Anstey, Eton, King's College, Cambridge, and, since 1784, barrister at law of Lincoln's Inn.

John Anstey is known to history through his entry in the Dictionary of National Biography as d. 1819 "poet"—his principal achievement having been the composition in 1796 of the "Pleaders Guide," a didactic poem containing the conduct and arguments of Counsellor Bore'um in an action between John-a-Gull and John-a-Gudgeon for assault and battery. His second achievement was to have published, in 1808, the complete works of his father, Christopher "Bath" Anstey, whose facility with Latin and mechanical ability with 18th century verse had earned him an immense reputation in his lifetime. John Anstey was, at the time of his death, commissioner for auditing public accounts.[2] William Smith, New York Loyalist then in London, met him on December 18, 1785 and noted that Anstey was "going out to New York Travelling Counsel to American Board." On a visit to Smith almost a month later Anstey stated that he wished "to be known as the Correspondent of the Board . . . and not as a Ministerial Agent or public Man. He lets out that his ultimate object however is to know the Country and be qualified for Office and Business here, in short to be qualified for a Place on the great Wheel. He means to be absent three years. . . ."[3]

Anstey set sail from Falmouth on February 19 1786 and arrived in New York City April 18. He had with him two servants and a secretary, Robert Woodruffe, who kept a journal. Finding the Coffee House too expensive for boarding "we paraded with a Concourse of People at our Heels to the City Tavern—in our way there we were informed that Mr. Anstey had been expected for some time—and Mr. Anstey was addressed by Mr. Rivington a Bookseller who sallied out from his shop for that purpose with a fulsome speech—Mr. Maule the gentleman who escorted us to the Tavern went so far as to say that the Government was a pack of Rascals . . . determined to ruin the Country." On the day following his arrival, Anstey visited the British Consul, John Temple, and the Governor of New York, George Clinton. Two days later he paid visits of respect to John Jay and other members of the Continental Congress. And then, on the 24th April, he dined with the Sons of St. George on their anniversary, drinking 15 toasts: to the King, Queen, Royal Family, the Governor of New York, the State of New

York, No Taxation without Representation, Universal Liberty.[4]

Anstey busied himself the rest of that first month with getting to know the leading figures in Congress and State. Jay received him with "Politeness and Respect" and promised the support of the "confederated Government," giving him letters of introduction to the governors of the various states. Anstey also heard expressions of surprise at the way the Loyalist Commissioners had distributed compensation to date, and amazement that the claims of the Loyalists ran so high.[5] He found that the names of many New York claimants were unknown in the state and everyone was so cordial to him that he became sure that many had left in a panic without any need to do so and had not tried hard enough to reassert their rights, instead, preferring to count on the generosity of the British Government. His new American friends also asserted that quite a few Loyalists had gained more than they had lost during the war, and, anyway, since it was they who had protracted the hostilities, why shouldn't they pay some of the extra costs involved? In New York at least "Animosities are in great measure subsided."[6] The "flattering reception" accorded him in the capital city of the nation boded ill for the Loyalists he would be investigating. But the more he learned and the further he travelled the more sympathetic he became to the objects of his enquiry.

Some of those who heard of his arrival rather naturally assumed that Commissioner Anstey had come to the United States to hear the claims of those unable to make their way to London. After all, commissioners had gone to British North America for that very purpose. Such hopefuls were among his first visitors in New York, but he had nothing to offer them, except to say that the time for lodging claims had passed.[7] The same thing happened elsewhere: in Philadelphia many Quakers, especially women and children, applied to him for help because they were too poor or infirm to go to Canada or England.[8] Others came with demands on the British government for losses inflicted by royal forces in foraging or commandeering transport and lodging.[9] But these claims also lay beyond Anstey's competence. Anstey had been instructed by the Loyalist Commissioners to gather all manner of documentary proofs relative to cases already under consideration, certified in such a way that the proofs would be admissible in a court of Law:

land title deeds; certificates of encumbrances; of debts satisfied out of claimants' estates; of the seizure of personal property; of the value of lands. He brought with him a catalogue of names of those individuals whose claims had been before the Commission; he had copied extracts from evidence books and decisions. From time to time he received express instructions to enquire into individual claims. He was to collect and transmit all the laws relating in any way to the loss of real and personal property.[10]

In addition to these duties, Anstey was also instructed to keep in touch with the commissioners in British North America, to send them copies of all relevant documents and to undertake specific enquiries at their command. Accordinly he announced his arrival in a letter addressed to them at St. John, but they were in Halifax. In May, the commissioners' secretary wrote an aggrieved letter to say that he had been notified of Anstey's arrival but had heard nothing from him.[11] When they did get in touch with each other, Anstey began to worry about the security of the documents he was sending off: their going astray was "a Hazard of too great Consequence to the main Success of the Business in which I am engaged" to be treated lightly.[12] The problem of communication continued as Anstey journeyed through the United States and the commissioners moved east from Halifax. Everything was apparently in order by June 1787 when Anstey, in Philadelphia, was sending material to the commissioners in Quebec.[13] The British American commissioners had enquiries of their own to make about the claimants who came before them: were they still living or holding property or office in the United States? Who exactly were the American officials who signed the certificates of loss that the claimants presented?[14] Anstey was responsible to two separate boards of commissioners.

As his New York friends assured him at the outset, the task was so immense that Anstey alone would take many years to complete it.[15] Anstey had given himself three years and kept to it. He left England in February 1786 and returned in September 1788. His journeying from London took him, by his own calculation, in excess of 15,000 miles. Until December 1786 he remained based at New York, with forays to Elizabethtown, Albany and Bennington in the outer darkness of Vermont. Then he decided to go south in the winter—before the heat got to be too much—and east in the summer—before the snows got too bad.[16] He visited Trenton, Philadelphia, Baltimore, Annapolis (in which he rented an office in January 1787), Richmond, Norfolk, New Bern, N.C. In April he moved his office to Philadelphia. In the winter of 1787 he was in Charleston and returned thence to New York city in April 1788 for the final phase.[17]

Travelling across the United States at that time was an arduous undertaking. Anstey intended to go in style. He rode in a four horse carriage brought from England with his servants as postilions. The carriage had a technological marvel unknown in America: headlights. When they were lit they "drew a large Concourse of People round us and in order to get rid of them we were obliged to put the lamps out and ride in the dark to the Hazard of being turned over every Step." But the good roads only went as far as Baltimore, where the carriage had to be left and the party proceed on horseback; Anstey and his secretary mounted, one servant leading a horse carrying the luggage and some provisions, the others sent with the rest of the luggage by stage to the next stop ahead.[18] The farther south, the worse things became. The party lost its way in woods and swamps where the track was covered in snow, and at Richmond Anstey decided to make further progress by water, a complicated precedure that required hiring boats as no passenger services were available.[19] When he failed to find a boat, Anstey tried to get to Charleston by land and after some 600 miles through to North Carolina was repulsed by the "overswelling of swamps." A kick from his horse didn't improve matters.[20]

Politics, as well as weather, affected the itinerary. By early 1787 Shay's Rebellion was causing alarms in Virginia which feared that its frontiers would be subject to attacks masterminded by Lord Dorchester in conjunction with the eastern rebels. "Foreigners of all Countries and Descriptions are looked upon with a very jealous and Suspicious Eye." Since "British emissaries" were supposedly the agents of these evil activities, Anstey's position was far from comfortable and his reception by Virginian officials downright surly. But the troubles also showed the wisdom of staying as far from New England for as long as possible, a part of the continent "very unfit to be resorted to by me." What should he do if the rebellion were still going on when the time came to visit there? How should he go to Vermont which was also supposedly in league with the rebels?[21] He delayed for as long as possible returning to the northeast until the middle of 1788.

Anstey hoped to gather information in much the same way as the London commissioners or, indeed, the commission that had gone to British North America. When he set up office in New York he envisaged people coming before him to give oral evidence and be cross-examined; the whole would be put in writing and attested to.[22] Accordingly he published an advertisement announcing his arrival and stating that his purpose was to acquire information for "liquidating the amount in value of the losses sustained" of claimants whose cases had already been presented in London. He could not, he emphasized, hear new claims. He would begin with those from the Southern District, and then present the names of the individual claimants (James De Lancey, Fredrick Philipse, Oliver De Lancey) and appoint a time when all interested persons "either as friends, relatives, or agents" would come to the office "to prove the titles of the claimants, or as creditors having demands on the estates confiscated . . ." or in any other capacity.[23] He soon discovered that no one was willing to swear to anything: he quickly realized that his investigations would encounter "the Passions and self Interests," and baffle "the secret Artifices of many, whose Credit and Fortune may eventually suffer . . . and whose Apprehensions have already taken the Alarm."[24] Yet he continued to advertise names of claimants until a letter from the London Board finally caught up with him in Philadelphia in April 1787.[25] But the information he required could not be obtained while sitting behind a desk in a rented office.

The first of many difficulties Anstey encountered was the basic one of finding out just what the laws were that related to the Loyalists. He apparently assumed that Congress would have copies of all state laws but was rapidly disabused of that notion. A search of the Secretary's Office for the relevant Laws of Massachusetts and Rhode Island failed to find them; and so it went with the other states. John Jay and Secretary Thompson wrote the governors of all the states, without much hope of success, and asked delegates from seven states for copies: again, nothing. Learning that Anstey was going south, Jay turned the tables on him by asking him to collect the laws to help Jay in making *his* report.[26] This Anstey did. In North Carolina he bought or copied whatever stray prints he found in shops and taverns along the way. Proclamations by the governor of South Carolina had disappeared and Anstey had nothing better than a borrowed press-clipping to go on.[27] Even in the better organised states of the north there were difficulties: Massachusetts was about to print up its laws but all the copies that actually existed had been printed solely for the private use of legislators after 1781 and those before that date were to be found only in newspapers.[28]

If it was difficult to find out what the law was, it was frequently impossible to find out where the documents were. The war was partly to blame. The records of Charlotte County, New York, were reputedly with Chief Justice Smith in Quebec, but they turned up in New City, Albany County.[29] Inquisitions into Loyalists in Virginia had been in a bag captured by General Arnold in 1781, which eventually found its way to the office of the clerk of the General Court, but some of the papers had been burned or used as waste, and no one knew how many.[30] The British had also carried off the records of Newport, R.I., in a ship that had been wrecked near Hell's Gate; after three months almost all the papers had been fished out.[31] In North Carolina documents of all descriptions were kept at the homes of the various officials. The comptroller general lived a hundred miles northwest of New Bern in nearly trackless bush and when Anstey finally got up his determination to make a visit, he found that the man had moved 200 miles farther inland. His efforts to learn something of the process of forfeiture in Dobb's County were ruined because the commissioner there "lay dangerously ill of a wound he had lately received in an Affray respecting the new federal Constitution."[32]

These occasional difficulties merely overlaid the basic problem of finding a way through the multiplicity of authorities Anstey had to consult: in Virginia, 82 counties, many of them created by subdivisions since the peace, and each having a clerk with its records; Anstey wouldn't put his faith in certified documents obtained through the post, but there was no post anyway.[33] In New York, there were 15 counties (2 revolted and joined Vermont), each with its court to register title deeds. The state secretary's office was supposed to have copies of all deeds but that could not be relied upon.

Most of the counties were split into four divisions, each with one or two Commisioners of Confiscation who held original documents.[34] North Carolina had seven districts, each with a supreme court, spread across its 700 mile breadth.[35] New Jersey, which, like North Carolina, had no one town that was "the Resort of the polite and opulent" nor center of judicial and executive business, also presented itself as a researcher's nightmare.[36]

Once the documents were found they had to be sorted and copied, and, if possible, provided with an affidavit as to their accuracy. The scope of the task may be seen from Anstey's collection of the names of those who had lost personal property in New York state. The names were copied from loose papers returned by the Commissioners of Sequestration to the State Auditor's Office: the papers were in no particular order and were copied as they came to hand. The clerks assured Anstey everything was correct but refused to take an oath to that effect.[37] The charges that accompanied copying were generally quite high and had to be accounted for and, since the paper available in the United States was of inferior quality, additional expense was incurred by having supplies sent out from England. Anstey was authorized to hire assistants to search and copy for him.[38] Samuel Bishop of New Haven must have been one of the best: he searched the records of Connecticut from 1755 to 1775, examining about 7,000 deeds and taking 65 extracts for a charge of only $13. Mr. Stockton of New Jersey was somewhat worried about the nature of his work and insisted on acting as Anstey's personal attorney rather than revealing any connection with any agency of the British government on his tour of the county clerks.[39]

One of the dangers of Anstey's research was that he might discover records of Loyalist estates that had somehow escaped the notice of the conspirators. Visiting Albany, he noted that the commisioners of forfeiture there were as eager to interview him as he was to talk to them.[40] In the case of Pennsylvania, claimants writing from London for complete certificates of loss had frequently revealed property that had not been confiscated through oversight, and then it promptly was.[41] Anstey feared that by making more "discoveries" he would not only be punishing the Loyalists by putting "such an Engine of Oppression in the Hands of the

State" but also increasing the amount of compensation Britain would be liable to pay.[42]

The question of compensation was in turn bound up with the question of land values, and Anstey did his best to cope with that problem: "I have long thought that the Opinion of Whigs as to the supposed Value of the Estates of the Tories a very unsafe and hollow Foundation for the Superstructure of substantial Justice."[43] What then was value? "The Answer is always in a Circle, it will bring as much as it is worth—and it is worth as much as it will bring." The Commissioners of Confiscation in Albany were housed in "a shop resembling a Hovel [with] a Stock Brokers office within, being the daily resort of speculating Dutchmen—the Value of the property fluctuating like the Stocks, according the Report of the Day."[44] The amount at which land had sold under confiscation was no guide, for in every state there had been collusive bidding, and even if this were not the case there might be special factors operating: in Pennsylvania, land had sold for less than its true value because the Quakers, "the most monied people . . . made it a Matter of Conscience not to purchase."[45] Then there was the matter of what sort of money had been paid for the lands: in Maryland they had been bought for specie—specie that was not hard, but paper money of "specie value"; red money; black money; State; Continental and Army Depreciation Certificates. All these moneys had to be explained and their depreciation charted, because the time of purchase would fix what the money was worth on the scale of depreciation: red money, for example, had depreciated 100% within three months of its issue in May 1781 but it had recovered and been paid off at par in hard money in June 1785. With money an impossible guide to value, Anstey resorted to his own assessments. He was much impressed with "navigation" as a mark of value: the bays and inlets of Maryland providing so much water-frontage that land was of fairly uniform value throughout.[46] In Maryland wooded land was more valuable than cleared land, but the reverse was true in Virginia. Since "navigation" was limited in Pennsylvania, the value of land near Philadelphia was exorbitantly high; but "navigation" did not save Newport, R.I., whose population had shrunk by 40% and "the grass grows on their Piers, which are in many Parts demolished and burst with the Tide . . . the

Wharves and the warehouses are empty and falling into ruins.''[47]

Anstey sent home reports on Massachusetts, New Hampshire, Rhode Island, New York, Pennsylvania, Delaware, Maryland, Virginia, North and South Carolina and Vermont. If there were reports on other states, they have not survived. He tried to follow a consistent pattern based on his first report — New York — proceeding through a number of topics: title to real property; the process of confiscation and sale; value of paper money and land; the sequestration of personal property; the treatment of debts. Along with each report he sent copies of the state laws and copies of whatever his researches had produced. To cite Maryland as one example, there were detailed reports on eleven individual claimants; a copy of the original book belonging to the commissioners for the sale of confiscated property (47 names), judgments of outlawry (10 names), alphabetical list of persons whose property was forfeited and sold (103 names), indictments for treason in 1781 (21 names), sales of confiscated property by the Intendant (71 names)—and much, much more.[48]

In the multiplicity of documents and names, large discrepancies appeared. One of the first sets of manuscript he attempted was the ''Schedule of Convictions in the State of New York'' wherein, he supposed, a confiscation had to be listed to be legal. He checked out the names with those on the list he had brought from London; of the 350 on his list, 208 had never been indicted while 85 were not indicted under the name on his list, but could be somebody else. In other words over 80% of the London claimants were not to be found in the schedule.[49] However, looking at the copy of all the convictions and indictments held by the clerk of the New York Supreme Court, he found 645 indictments, of which 595 had been carried through to judgment. Yet another list found in the office of the Commissioners of Forfeiture contained 500 names not to be found amongst the London claimants—two-thirds of the total. A total of 1022 Loyalists appeared to have lost personal property (this report carried an affidavit from the state Auditor General).[50] And so Anstey entered a bewildering numbers game, and at the same time swelled the pigeon holes of the London commissioners.

His reports tried to sort out these confusions as they occurred state after state. If a claimant's name did not appear on the official lists it could mean that he was claiming land to which he had no title or to which his title was too imperfect to justify seizure, or that the state had not yet discovered his lands, or that the record had been lost. The London commissioners would have to decide. And there was more than one way to lose property: many in the war zones had abandoned possessions with the ebb and flow of the armies, and so lost them forever. Various laws, not confiscatory by name, had the same effect, for example, the New York Trespass Act of 1783.[51] The 1784 Restoration Act of South Carolina ostensibly allowed Loyalists to get their property back, but when all the procedures were followed, the individual might expect a maximum of 8% of its true value. In fact there were six times as many South Carolina claimants as were recorded by the state as suffering loss: many of the rest were probably speculators in western land who had been unable to complete their titles in time during the war or in the six month grace period allowed all holders in 1784. These Loyalists had lost land not because they were loyal, but because they were not in the state at the right time, but they were not in the state at the right time *because* they had been loyal.[52] In Pennsylvania some eighty claimants did not appear on the state's lists but could have lost property through non-payment of taxes, at a time when such payment would have been an overt act of treason against the King.[53] And so it went, state by state, as the London commissioners were educated in the complexities of state politics.

Anstey had expressed some doubts about the Loyalists in his early days in New York, but his reservations disappeared as he looked into the motives of those who had despoiled them and many times he recommended that the claimants be given the benefit of the doubt. The commissioners of confiscation and sequestration were universally said to be guilty of embezzlement, often by minimising the value of the property on their returns which they themselves had bought. In South Carolina the confiscation lists had to be redrawn six times, as "almost every Man had his personal Enemies" to place on the roll.[54] The laws of Massachusetts were so complex that "it requires a Degree of Discernment" to understand them "equal at least to the Art and Ingenuity of those who framed them" and enforced them in "so complicated and contradictory" a manner. The only key to understanding what happened was to remember that since those who framed the laws also executed them, the state itself hardly received anything from "the Downfal and Extirpation of the most opulent Families."[55] Of all the states New York was accorded the honour of being the most regular in its proceedings, conforming to the principle of legislation in its frame, and to Common Law in its practice. The sale of confiscated property, however, remained an important prop to the state's shaky financial system.[56] New Jersey, the cockpit of the war, had used confiscation to prevent defections to the King's army and not as a way of filling its treasury.[57] The object in Virginia had been to repudiate European creditors; property had been seized under the "colour of sequestring and preserving in Trust" and debts extinguished by "a Master Stroke of political Swindling."[58] Even though the motive for action against the Loyalists had varied from state to state, the execution of the laws had everywhere been in the spirit of plunder.

Generally speaking these animosities were things of the past. Anstey and his mission were received without rancor. He met a number of dignitaries who, given their war record, might have shunned him. George Washington, in retirement at Mt. Vernon, was proud to show Anstey a prize jackass given him by the King of Spain.[59] Governor William Livingston of New Jersey (himself a versifier when a young law student) received him hospitably.[60] President Samuel Adams of the Massachusetts Senate was still hostile to Loyalists, but then Adams never had thought "with the Generality of Mankind upon any subject . . . the prevailing Sentiments are not unfavourable to the Loyalists in that State."[61] Perhaps the attitude in Virginia best summed up the situation: "the whole Concern of the Loyalists . . . except as to Prosecutions for private Purposes of Injustice by Individuals in Power, has totally fallen asleep, and is finished, and no one concerns himself to talk about confiscated Property."[62] Only North Carolina which ironically had passed an Act of Pardon and Oblivion in 1783 was still confiscating property and holding criminal prosecutions in defiance of the Peace Treaty, but these activities may have been simply the result of conditions there, "the Barbarity of the New Settlers, [and] the Scarcity of Law in general."[63] In most cities there were examples of individual Loyalists who had returned and resumed life unmolested; even in the towns of Rhode Island several lived "in as much Credit with the World as any of the most violent and determined Whig Citizens of that refractory Commonwealth . . . can expect."[64]

For the future, Anstey had only moderate expectations of the new federal constitution. He was in Philadelphia while the debates were proceeding but did not report on them. However, he did note in connection with South Carolina, that the judicial power of the new government would extend to controversies between a state and foreign citizens and it would be possible for a Loyalist to bring suit to recover the original value of lands "but this Foundation lies too deep and too remote to be built upon." There were many obstacles to be overcome: how could states unable to support one government be expected to maintain two?[65]

Anstey provided the Loyalist commissioners with twenty volumes of material. They were properly appreciative. "We must remark the material assistance we have derived from the enquiries of John Anstey, Esq" noted the Twelfth Report, for he had provided the information without which most cases could not have been completed. His work, wrote Wilmot, "contributed much to aid the honest, to detect the fraudulent, or to correct the mistaken Claimant; but more especially enabled the Commissioners to do justice to many, who would not otherwise have been able to substantiate their claims." The Loyalist commissioners could now move from payments on account to final settlement: between 1785 and 1787 they had awarded £1,462,977.4.0.[66] That is the measure of the importance of the mission of John Anstey.

THE IMPERIAL DIMENSION
British Ministerial Perspectives During the American Revolutionary Crisis, 1763–1776

BY

IAN CHRISTIE

═══════════════

THE inclusion in this collection of essays of a paper which does not concern itself directly with the situations and the ideas of the Loyalists may perhaps be justified on the ground that the perspectives considered in it formed a significant element of the context in which loyalist attitudes and motivations gradually evolved in the years of crisis surrounding the Declaration of Independence. No doubt many Loyalists were drawn to take their stand by simple considerations of personal sentiment or interest and never came near to rationalizing their loyalism in terms of the complex and sophisticated concepts of empire current among those men in London whose business it was to direct the Empire's affairs. In times of political stress political reflection and speculation are often confined to immediate issues, fail to rise above specific controversies, and ignore the wider implications of the situations under debate. This was as true of Loyalists as it was of Patriots or of the British participants in the Anglo-American crisis. Nevertheless, the question must arise how far the views held in London, radiating outwards through the courts of the various colonial governors and by the efforts of those who acted as propagandists on their behalf, permeated and influenced those circles of colonial society where loyalism was eventually to find expression. The following sketch of these views may suggest further lines of enquiry into the nature of loyalism.

I

During the winter of 1913-14 the future historian, Sir Lewis Namier, then a young man in business in New York, consulted Charles McLean Andrews about the study he proposed to undertake on "The Imperial Problem during the American Revolution." Andrews pointed out to him that much work on the American side of the question was being done in America and, emphasizing the gap that needed to be filled, he asked: "Why do you not contribute something from your own side?" Fifteen years afterwards Namier redefined the nature of the question, in the preface to the first fruits of that seminal interview, his book, *The Structure of Politics at the Accession of George III.* There he wrote, "as the conflict of 1775 was more closely connected with everyday life in the American colonies than in this country, America [had] by now entered as a community into the picture of the Revolution, while Great Britain [remained] more or less the figure on our copper coins." The "notion of this country in the conflict," he went on, "needed to be humanized."[1]

This analysis pointed to two lines of approach only one of which Namier opened up, and that only partially: first, the presentation of the flesh and blood personalities of the British political actors during the American crisis; second, a narrative in the fullest detail of the interplay between the formulation of policy decisions and the political activity in the Commons and the corridors of power at Whitehall. Since the last war there has been a fair amount of scholarly progress in both these directions. Rounded form has been given to many of the actors on the British political stage in the multi-volume work inspired and largely executed by Namier, the later 18th century section of the *History of Parliament.* A number of close analyses of the formulation and execution of British policy have been written on the basis of the departmental records, most of these, with a few recent exceptions, being by American scholars. One or two—but not enough—British cabinet ministers of the period have been studied biographically with due examination of their concern with the problems of the empire. Also some attention has been given to the intellectual premises and the circumstantial considerations underlying British policy.

Although much further investigation is still required, historians are moving towards a situation in which they can discard the image of Britannia as an abstract entity from which emanated tyrannous blows, or as an embodiment of corruption battening on the colonial body politic. These are stereotypes of the enemy on the other side of the hill, which entered deeply into the American revolutionary tradition and of which the faint ghosts still occasionally haunt the literature today. It is becoming increasingly possible to replace these stereotypes with accounts of individuals and bodies of men in Great Britain who were responsible in varying degrees for formulating decisions and taking action according to the best lights available to them and under all the terrifying limitations of human fallibility. To move in this direction is to take an important step towards a fuller understanding of one of the most important events in the history of modern western civilization.

The task of humanizing the British side of the American crisis involves entering more closely into the thinking of the men who were responsible in the broadest sense for conducting colonial affairs. This requies penetration at two levels in the political hierarchy: first, that of the secretaries of state in charge of the colonies and their officials, and also of the other cabinet ministers whose influence or concurrence in colonial affairs was important; and second, that of the general body of members of Parliament in both Houses, whose preconceptons, predilections and prejudices had to be wooed and respected by the ministers. In the present context I am not concerning myself with trains of thought and argument connected with British decisions on immediate particular questions. These have been worked out by many historians in considerable detail, and a very full though not altogether agreed-upon story of events has already emerged in the monograph literature. But much of this detailed work has not yet been placed in general perspective. As yet it is hardly possible to see the wood for the trees. Hence my concern in this paper with the general British over-view on various major questions, so far as this can be gathered from what ministers and peers and Members of Parliament said and wrote.

To some extent the different elements of this over-view can be classified as a series of preoccupations standing in an ascending order of importance, although the interconnections between the different categories are intimate and often difficult to untangle. If we adopt this approach, it seems to me that the following questions can successively be examined: What general plan did the ministers have in mind for the American part of the British empire in the years after the Peace of Paris of 1763? What were their views about the function of empire, and to what general lines of attack on their problems did these views lead them? What light does this throw, so far as the British side is concerned, on the vital argument over the supreme powers of the imperial authorities?

II

In this survey it is natural to start with those ministerial perspectives which are most clearly established and familiar. In the early part of George III's reign ministers had a general view regarding the immediate further development of the North American provinces. This view was most clearly articulated in the period immediately after 1763 when policy was set down in two major public instruments, the Proclamation of 1763 establishing government in the newly-conquered territories and the Plantation Act (commonly called the Sugar Act) of 1764. If it is not so directly traceable later on, this does not mean that the lines of action then laid down did not continue to dominate ministerial thinking. On the contrary, continued adherence to them was often clearly implicit in the actions and utterances of British public men.

From 1763 onwards, with a fair degree of consistency though with little success, governments sought to divert expansion in North America away from the west and into the less populated or empty areas to the north and south of the old colonies. This policy rested upon both positive and negative arguments. A strong build-up of white Anglo-Saxon Protestants in the valley and estuary of the St.

Lawrence might open up agricultural and fishery resources and even some mineral wealth, and would provide a counterpoise to the Roman Catholic French-speaking inhabitants of Quebec, whose loyalty was bound to remain doubtful, at least for a time. At the southern extremity of the continent, Georgia was still scantily populated and the newly-conquered Floridas were almost empty. These areas were thought of as valuable potential sources of Mediterranean-type and subtropical crops. Moreover, it was patently obvious to ministers how inadvisable it would be to leave extensive territories unpopulated within easy striking distance of Spanish bases at New Orleans and Havana.

On the negative side, ministers and officials generally believed that settlements west of the Alleghanies were undesirable. Difficulties of communication were expected to render any economic connection between Great Britain and the inland provinces tenuous if not non-existent. It was also anticipated that this circumstance might force such colonies into manufacturing for themselves, and so introduce a new unwanted competition for the markets of the tidewater provinces.[2]

One minister, the Earl of Shelburne, during the years 1766-67 displayed some enthusiasm for inland settlements as a means of solving the problem of western security, but this appears as an aberration in the general picture. Although two or three other ministers became involved a little later on with schemes for settlement in the Ohio valley, it seems right to conclude that their activity was connected more with political infighting within the government than with any genuine interest in such plans. The opposing view, that the interior should be left to the Red Indians, was strongly represented by such leading politicians as the veteran Lord Halifax, who had been president of the board of trade throughout the 1750s, the Earl of Egremont, who was primarily responsible for shaping the Proclamation of 1763, and the Earl of Hillsborough who became in 1768 the first secretary of state in charge of the colonies as a separate department. In addition to their opposition to inland settlements on the grounds outlined above, these men had a genuine concern for the interests of the Red Indian population in the wilderness and sought, though not very successfully, to protect them.

III

Underpinning these ideas about the direction of settlement and economic development in North America after 1763 lay broader concepts about the nature and purpose of empire which carried other implications for the formulation of policy. These concepts, which had been elaborated by theorists and encapsulated in legislation during the late-seventeenth century, exercised a powerful attraction upon the minds of those in authority in mid-eighteenth century Britain.[3] For example, it is hardly coincidence that the influential *Discourses* on public revenue and trade of Charles Davenant first published in the 1690s, were reprinted in 1771— reprinted, moreover, in a new edition of his works prepared by Sir Charles Whitworth, M.P., formerly a backbencher attached to the Duke of Newcastle, who by the 1770s was occupying a key position as chairman of the committee of ways and means in the House of Commons. Excellent evidence for the impact of these theories during the 1760s is to be found in the writings of the government official, Thomas Whately, who as George Grenville's secretary to the treasury was very closely in his confidence and therefore intimately involved in the working out of government policy.

Colonial theory, as it had evolved during the century up to 1760, posited that colonies and metropolis naturally formed a closed economic system for mutual benefit, in which the former furnished raw materials, strategic materials, and exotic goods, while the latter provided manufactures and financial backing. There was a corrosive element in this pattern of thought, pregnant with disastrous psychological consequences, the impact of which has often been noticed by historians of the American Revolution, though its deep-rooted character has been less often the subject of comment. From an early stage in the history of the empire, metropolitan attitudes were colored by the belief that colonies had been created simply for economic advantage and must be continuously managed to this end. The seventeenth-century East India Company magnate and writer on commercial matters, Sir Josiah Child, expressed the opinion that "all colonies or plantations do endamage their mother kingdoms, whereof the trades of such plantations are not confined by severe laws and good execution of those laws to the mother kingdom."[4] The political economist, Charles

Davenant, laid down that "colonies are a strength to their mother kingdoms while they are under good discipline . . . But otherwise they are worse than members lopped from the body politic."[5] When Thomas Wately of the treasury wrote in 1764 that "colonies are only settlements made in distant parts of the world, for the improvement of trade," he reflected the general mid-eighteenth century subscription to the basic tenet underlying these seventeenth century dicta.[6]

The primary implication of this mode of thought was that the imperial government must ultimately determine what courses of economic action were in the general interest of the nation. The secondary implication was one which, with the greatest goodwill, it was almost impossible for the imperial government to avoid in practice, and one which peripheral communities of the nation would inevitably come to believe in theory—that is, that in clashes between the interests of the colonies and the mother country, the former would be treated as expendable. Once this state of mind had come into being, the extent to which the situation supposed to exist would be tolerated would be partly determined by the degree of dependence upon the centre felt by the peripheral communities. Here of course lay the great distinction in the 1770s between the North American provinces and the British West Indian colonies.

IV

Here a consideration arises that perhaps deserves more attention than it has received. A point of growing importance during the 1760s was that breaches of the closed economic system were seen in Whitehall both as an indirect threat to national security and as a violation of the basic principles on which the national prosperity rested. British suspicions (justified or not) about colonial trading with the enemy during the recent war may have helped to draw attention to this issue, but British policy was based on much wider considerations. When the British treasury team was engaged in reshaping trade regulations during 1763 and 1764—an unsettling activity to the colonies when it emerged in various clauses of the Plantation Act of 1764—the responsible members envisaged an essentially dual task: to foster the economic resources of the empire, and to deny other powers any advantages from it. In his pamphlet, *The Regulations lately made concerning the colonies and the taxes imposed on them considered,* Thomas Whately defended the Act:[7]

> To encourage the consumption of our own produce and our own manufactures, in preference to those of other countries, has been at all times an undisputed maxim of policy; and for this purpose high duties and even prohibitions have been laid upon foreign commodities, while bounties have been granted on our own. The general tendency of the Act . . . is to extend the same principle to the American, as is followed in respect to our home trade and consumption.

In another passage he also observed that "it is the policy of every nation to prohibit all foreign trade with their plantations."[8]

Two further points deserve emphasis in this context. One is the treasury's attempt to plan for the general economic benefit. While concerned to dampen any tendency of the colonies to become competitors with British manufacturers, the men who set the new course in policy during the 1760s believed in doing this by means of the carrot, not the stick. Further legislative restrictions on colonial enterprise such as the Hat Act or the Iron Act were not considered advisable or even worth while. It was probably understood that the Iron Act remained a dead letter in America. Their approach respecting the trade in linens, for example, as Whately explained it, was on the one hand to ensure that British prices were kept competitive, and on the other to encourage by bounty colonial export of the raw material so that there would be less incentive to put it to use in manufacture in America. These processes of adjustment could involve sacrifices among subjects of George III in Britain as well as in the colonies. In the general imperial interest the government was prepared in 1764 to run down and extinguish a British whale fishery based at Poole in Dorset, on the grounds that imperial needs for whale products could be met more cheaply and efficiently by a local whale fishery based in the area of New England,

Nova Scotia, and the St. Lawrence estuary.[9]

The other point deserving emphasis in this connection is the imperial government's assumption that to an important extent commerce was merely warfare pursued by other means. This consideration arose particularly over relations with Britain's great continental rival, the kingdom of France. Throughout the eighteenth century—except for a brief interval inaugurated later by the Eden commercial treaty of 1786—the British, using high tariffs and prohibitions, systematically tried to deny to the French any benefits of mutual trade. With the signing of the peace treaty in 1763, this preoccupation moved once more to the forefront. Trade statistics give clear evidence of its effect. In the early 1770s lawful British exports to France, having edged up from the wartime zero of 1763, were estimated to be running at the insignificant annual value of slightly under £100,000. This was about one-fifth of the value of British export trade to Portugal, a British ally but a far smaller country than France, about one-tenth of the trade to the Austrian Netherlands and less than a tenth of that to either the Dutch Netherlands or the German states.[10] It is in the light of this situation that historians need to assess the impact of George Grenville's suspicions, disclosed to the House of Commons in March 1764, that "three or four" colonies were conducting a direct trade with France to the amount of £4 or £500,000 per annum—that is to say, were carrying on an illicit traffic many times more extensive than the lawful trade which was permitted to subjects living in Great Britain.[11]

Smuggling, of course, meant loss of revenue, but this was only a small part of the matter. More important, Britain was being deprived of economic benefits inherent in her position as metropolis, and the potential enemy, France, was receiving direct benefit instead. Thomas Whately in a passage of his pamphlet quoted above, left his readers in no doubt that the government found this reprehensible. If colonies traded freely with foreign countries, he wrote, they "would destroy the very purpose of their establishment," and divert the wealth channeled into them by their parent state to the enrichment of its rivals. On the contrary, the duty of members of the British nation overseas was clear: "They, the subjects still of the same country, should continue to act as they must have acted, had they continued its inhabitants, and . . . their produce and their consumption should be for the benefit of that country in preference to any other.'' Colonies which traded illicitly with foreign states were ''no longer *British* colonies, but colonies of the country they traded to.''[12]

The implication was clear. Once eliminate the supreme central imperial authority having full power to enforce its policies, and such a situation would be irremediable. How far the British government was justified in its suspicions about the extent of the illegal traffic between the colonies and various countries of the European Continent remains a question on which the last word has yet to be said. Current conflicting opinions among historians may perhaps be resolvable by fuller investigation of such European port archives as escaped the rain of fire in the 1940s. But the suspicions were there and formed part of the general perspective of ministers and of politicians in Parliament when they considered colonial affairs. This is at least part of the explanation why no British government after 1765 made any concessions over those parts of the Sugar Act of 1764 which reinforced the Navigation Acts and the Acts of Trade—not even over those most unpopular instruments of enforcement, the courts of vice-admiralty.

The element of economic warfare also revealed itself in particular aspects of Grenville's commercial policy. The molasses duty of 1764 was expected to fall on the French West India planters, not on the British North American colonists, and was intended to reduce the capacity of the planters to compete in the world market against the British West India sugar producers by putting up their costs and reducing their ancillary profits. It was believed in Whitehall that the North American traders in molasses were in a sufficiently dominant economic position to pass on practically the whole incidence of the duty, thus virtually acting as no more than tax collectors. Similarly, taxes on wines imported into the colonies from Madeira and the Canaries were intended to squeeze the producers who had grown fat on their virtual monopoly. The treasury expected that, overall, wines would become cheaper in America than before.[13] But for the post-war economic depression of the mid 1760s, political distortion of trade relationships, and the British tax concessions of 1766, the government's views on these matters might perhaps have been proved accurate by events.

V

Behind these British considerations regarding the direction of colonial economic development and the control of trade there lay a still more embracing over-view of the nature and the role of the empire as an entity in world affairs.

In the first place, there was a widely diffused belief in the essential unity of the community of British people wherever they might dwell. This concept in its most general form was not confined to public men in Great Britain alone: it can be found, for instance, in the early writings of John Adams and Benjamin Franklin.[14] In Whitehall and Westminster this assumption generated a sense of responsibility for and among all the subjects of King George, whether in Great Britain or in America, who were considered as sharing the same privileges and responsibilities as well as the same obligations. Writing in defence of George Grenville's colonial policy at the end of 1764, his confidant, Thomas Whately, phrased it thus:[15]

> The *British* empire in *Europe* and in *America* is still the same power. Its subjects in both are still the same people; and all equally participate in the adversity or prosperity of the whole. Partial advantages that opposed the general good would finally be detrimental to the particulars who enjoyed them. The mother country would suffer, if she tyrannized over her colonies: the colonies would decline, if they distressed their mother country: for each is mutually important to the other, and mutual benefits, mutual necessity cement their connexion.

It was the logical progression from this vision of empire that opened a gulf between British in Great Britain and British in America. To men in public life in the metropolitan state—to practically all members of both Houses of Parliament and to the men who served in court and government offices—the fact of single nationhood inexorably carried with it the subordination of all to a single source of authority. This seemed to them to be on the one hand fully embodied in the law and practice of the constitution, and on the other both necessary and inherently natural. The distinguished jurist, Sir William Blackstone, a Member of Parliament during the 1760s, wrote without reservation of "the general superintending power of the legislature in the mother country" and of the subordination of the colonies to the laws which it passed.[16] That practical politician, Thoms Whately, wrote in continuation of his analysis of the relationship of the colonies and the parent state:

> It is an indisputable consequence of their being thus one nation, that they must be govern'd by the same supreme authority, be subject to one executive power in the king, to one legislative power in the Parliament of *Great Britain*. Their connexion would otherwise be an alliance, not a union; and they would be no longer one state but a confederacy of many.[17]

While agreeing that local authorities were natural and proper bodies to look after local concerns, Whately stressed that there were many general questions affecting the whole empire which could only be regulated by the central legislative authority constituted by the British Parliament. Parliamentary supremacy, he wrote, "appears from hence to be founded not only upon just right, but upon absolute necessity." This was a proposition with which few British Americans had had occasion to quarrel before 1760, because up to that time there had been little need for them to look at the small print. In the early 1760s James Otis junior presumably reflected the orthodox, educated, colonial lawyers' opinions. There is no conflict between Whately's assertion of principle quoted above and Otis's own observation in his pamphlet, *The Rights of the British Colonies Asserted and Proved,* that "a supreme legislature and a supreme executive power must be placed somewhere in every commonwealth."[18]

Of course, when British colonial policy after 1763 pushed the colonists into a detailed examination of exactly what this proposition implied, they soon came to the conclusion, that, since Parliament was a body in which they had no direct representation, its role as a supreme legislature must be rejected. Two main considerations drove them in this direction. They felt (whether correctly or not) seriously incommoded in their economic activity by the action taken by the "supreme legislature and supreme executive power." Even more important, they came to believe that the more extended use of these powers was overturning the whole constitution and fabric of political society as they understood it.

British politicians were constantly informed of these circumstances but were always unwilling to concede the point of substance. Why was this so?

VI

A constitutional dogma had become branded on the minds of people in Great Britain that Parliament had a supreme authority. Thoughtful individuals on both sides of the Atlantic might toy with expedients by which its representative character and thereby its command of confidence among the colonists might be improved; but few were convinced that the system needed recasting and their suggestions attracted only the most perfunctory attention from the politicians. In 1765 the Connecticut agent Jared Ingersoll set out for Governor Fitch an admirable reconstruction of the prolonged dialogue between George Grenville and the colonial agents. He represented the British minister as admitting that Parliament's lack of contact with colonial society involved "inconveniences," but as observing at the same time that it was difficult to see how even the allocation of seats in the Commons to colonial representatives could overcome this, in view of the expense and the difficulties of communication involved.[19]

With such a reform not regarded as practical politics, the exposition of the theory of virtual representation published in 1765 by Grenville's supporters was an alternative, unsuccessful, ministerial attempt to rationalize the supremacy of Parliament—one so little attuned to realities in the colonies that nothing more was heard of it. By 1766, with the passage of the Declaratory Act affirming Parliament's full power to legislate for the colonies in all cases whatsoever, the politicians, as Edmund S. Morgan has said, "had retreated to the heights of arbitrary declaration."[20] However, this was done not simply because the supremacy of Parliament had become a constitutional dogma, but because so much appeared to depend upon it.

According to Jared Ingersoll's account already cited, if the American rejection of Parliament's authority in matters of taxation were to be admitted, then George Grenville believed that one of two possible consequences appeared to follow: either Britain and America "must . . . be two distinct kingdoms and that now immediately," or America "must . . . be defended entirely by us."[21]

The second of these points needs only brief consideration, though it is not without significance. Owing to the sequence of events after 1774, only the short-term implications of it ever became clear. In practice the maintenance of defence forces in America did fall almost entirely upon the British exchequer between 1764 and 1775. As a proportion of the total budget the amount was relatively small—perhaps five or six per cent—and the proportion Grenville had proposed to shift on to the backs of the colonists was less than two per cent. This was not an unbearable burden, but it was enough to create resentment. There is plenty of evidence to show that this rankled in the minds of British politicians of all descriptions who were conscious of crushing expenditures incurred in the war that had cleared the French from the backs of the colonists and of continued heavy taxation since the signing of the peace. Policy towards the colonists was therefore influenced to some extent by a gut reaction of the most elementary kind—as raw and natural as the famous taunt attributed to President Coolidge against the defaulting European nations in the 1920s: "They hired the money didn't they?" Although one historian has recently suggested that there is some doubt in the matter, it nevertheless seems very likely that in 1767 it was this emotional current running through the House of Commons which led to the passage of Charles Townshend's Revenue Act.[22] Only a group of strong-minded ministers guided by firm convictions could have held the ring against this emotional pressure, and there were no such men in office, at any rate after 1766.

But it was the first of the alternatives posited by Grenville that most shocked the nerves of the British politicians. Despite all the colonists' perfectly genuine disclaimers of any intention to seek independence from the British connection, politicians at the center of empire persisted in believing that independence would be the situation in fact, unless the supremacy of Parliament was recognized and seen to be working. From the viewpoint of London the logic of the argument that the abandonment of executive and legislative control over the colonies would in effect mean American independence from Great Britain, even if on friendly terms, was difficult to refute; and such a consummation was awful to contemplate. Some Englishmen, in relaxed and private moments, might admit that a greatly developed American dominion could not possibly be retained forever in leading strings, but every consideration led them to thrust this spectre of independence as far as possible from them into the uncertain and distant future.

The primary compulsion shaping their attitude lay in the general political circumstances of the Atlantic world. British statesmen saw themselves as engaged in cut-throat competition with other similar empires for their place in the sun. In particular they feared the pressures from France. France appeared to be dowered in Europe with more than double the potential in territory, population and natural resources of Great Britain itself. Moreover, France was linked by the Bourbon family compact with the other remaining great empire in the New World. British cabinets were constantly preoccupied with this problem. A series of minor and major international crises involving Britain and France studded the years from 1763 to 1773, and in general British ministries were concerned throughout to show by constant sabre-rattling that they would proceed to extremes in any emergency. On a number of these occasions the British were worried about the possibilities of a French preemptive strike at sea, or of a fundamental displacement of the balance of power in her favour. This explains British nervousness in 1768 over the French occupation of Corsica, and the diplomatic pressure backed by naval threats employed against France at certain stages of the Russo-Turkish war of 1768-74, and in the Swedish crisis of 1772-3. The Falkland Islands crisis of 1770-71 was not only a direct confrontation with Spain about open access to the South Pacific, but also a test of French intentions.

This situation of international tension had various implications for British handling of the American question.

In the first place, it exerted an immediate impact at particular times. It could impose a direct check on the unfolding of coercive policies. There seems little doubt that something in the nature of the Massachusetts Government Act of 1774 was postponed in the winter of 1770-71 owing to the Falkland Islands crisis and again in the early months of 1773 by the Swedish imbroglio.[23] Had there been another international crisis in the winter of 1773-74, it seems probable that the affair of the Boston Tea Party would have blown over without the aftermath of the Coercive Acts and all their consequences.

In the second place, tensions with France and Spain kept up British concern about a strategic presence in the New World. If ministers in the capital ever overlooked this, the expert on the spot was quick to remind them. In the quiet summer of 1771 following the Falkland Islands crisis, the government contemplated withdrawing five regiments from North America, partly for economy, partly to reinforce the home garrison. General Gage, the British commander-in-chief at New York, who a few months before had been contemplating the likelihood of a Spanish onslaught on West Florida, pointed out that this step would leave him with no mass of reserve in case of any future emergency.[24] Nothing more was heard of this proposal.

In the third place, the constant tension kept alive concern with the general build-up of British imperial strength, both economic and military, and in particular of the economic power inherent in the system embodied in the long series of Acts of Trade and Navigation running right up to the Rockingham ministry's Plantation Act of 1766. In the existing international situation the British nation, enjoying full and integrated command of the resources both of the British Isles and of eastern North America, might be confidently expected to hold its own. There was much less certainty that this would be the case if the war potential and the sources for economic conflict at the nation's disposal ceased to be under the effective control of a single supreme government. In March 1776 one ministerial supporter in the House of Lords, the Earl of Carlisle, expressed the fear that if control over America were lost, Great Bri-

tain would sink into obscurity and insignificance, falling at length
"a prey to the first powerful or ambitious state, which [might]
meditate a conquest of this island."[25] There was fear also that an
America which was left to go it alone would soon be swallowed up
by the Bourbon empires or would at least fall into a state of client-
age to them—almost the worst possible of all consequences, since it
would transfer the formidable resources of the colonies into the
hands of the powers regarded as Great Britain's most dangerous
rivals. Imperial unity was identified with national safety. This was
one of the most compelling elements in the British perspective during the American revolutionary crisis.

VII

The historian's search for understanding involves in principle
the widest possible investigation of every relevant aspect of the
problems before him. In dealing with the American Revolution this
process entails examination of the activities and motives not only of
the makers of the Revolution in America, but of the Loyalists,
whose visions were destroyed in the clash of arms, and also of the
imperial authorities. But for the actions of these last there would
have been no revolution. Analysis of the intellectual and emotional
premises of the British politicians is therefore an essential part of
the task of achieving a full understanding of that cataclysmic event.

It is clear that, broadly speaking, despite all vacillations of
policy arising from changes of administration between 1763 and
1776, British public men shaped American measures within the
confines of certain broad guidelines and concepts which they all
more or less clearly accepted. They believed that the exploitation of
the empire's resources required deliberate planning. They considered that—at least in certain areas where the nation's interests
seemed to dictate this—a system of commercial monopoly should
be maintained, entailing a considerable amount of commercial
direction and regulation. They were driven in this direction by their
understanding of the nature of international pressures and threats
to national security. In dealing with this situation it appeared to
them that control of trade and natural resources constituted an im-

portant economic weapon against dangerous rivals. These considerations in themselves pointed to the necessity for a continuing
single supreme authority within the empire. This circumstance reinforced an assumption based on inheritance from the past, that all
members of the British nation, whether living in Great Britain or in
America, belonged to a single state and were subordinate to the
single direct superintendending power of King in Parliament. Not
only did the imperial institutions have to be there; they were present
in actuality as a result of the historical development of the British
constitution. National safety dictated that their existence should be
preserved and their operation made more effective. In the strength
conferred by this institutional unity lay the nation's security,
whereas the dissolution of the empire into a confederacy of unar-
ticulated, associated states promised disaster. (Indeed, the contin-
uance of such an anarchic system appeared to presage disaster in
the view of the American Federalists after 1783. In many respects
the preoccupations of the Federalist writers in 1787-88 paralleled
those of Grenville in the 1760s.)[26] Historians seeking the fullest
possible understanding of a crucial episode in Western history need
to explore these themes and to incorporate them in the general narrative of the American revolutionary crisis.

THE POSSIBILITIES FOR QUANTITATIVELY-ORIENTED RESEARCH ON THE LOYALISTS IN CANADA

With Specific Examples from "A Study of New Brunswick 'Loyalist' Society, 1783 to 1815."*

BY

JO-ANN FELLOWS

===

I believe that it is now possible to carry out studies which can answer the following questions about the communities that the Loyalist exiles of the American Revolution established in certain areas of what later became Canada, i.e., the provinces of Ontario, New Brunswick and, to a lesser extent, Nova Scotia. How many Loyalists came to Canada? Where did they settle, and how? What was their age, sex, marital state and size of family on arrival? What were the basic demographic details, through time, of the societies that they established, or, in the case of Nova Scotia, helped to establish—their marriage, birth and death rates, their marriage patterns, family size, birth spacings, etc.—the details that D. V. Glass has called "the facts of life"?[1] After the details of demography and settlement are determined, a great deal of analytical and comparative work is possible and interpretations already proposed can be tested. Ultimately, it is hoped that an approach from the viewpoint of historical demography will yield new interpretations for this period in Canadian history.

*Acknowledgement is made of Canada Council Grants S73-1098 and S74-1090, that partially supported this research.

For the past two years, I have been devoting at least part of my time to a quantitatively-oriented study of New Brunswick "Loyalist" society, that is, of the population of New Brunswick from 1783 to 1815.[2] I am listing, coding and machine-entering all nominal records for the province in this period. With the use of record linkage,[3] the information from the various records will be combined. I then intend to produce a census for the population of the province.[4]

The study is inclusive, and Loyalists, although they were by far the largest single group in the province in this period, will be joined by the Acadians, the Early-English settlers, and, where possible, by the Indians. Loyalty and the details of Revolutionary War service will be entered as variables among others describing the individual. Then, simple, descriptive statistics for the entire population and its constituent groups will be produced, and, finally, more complex statistical techniques will be applied where useful.

Initially, the emphasis in the compiling of data is on land records, since these are the largest and most important collections of data in this period. Land and its settlement is the major obsession of the period.[5] Land petitions, land grants and cadestral maps provide these data, along with deeds, and wills when they mention land, which they usually do. A register of Loyalists has also been discovered for the 1783 to 1785 period with annotations up to 1792.[6] It resembles the land board records maintained in Upper Canada during the period of Loyalist settlement. It lists Loyalists who were granted land, locates the land, indicates whether they actually settled their land, and if they did not take up their land, or abandoned it, indicates where they went, such as "deceased," "went to Upper Canada," "returned to United States," etc. Additionally, a list of Loyalists published in 1956 as an Appendix to E.C. Wright's *The Loyalists of New Brunswick*.[7] will be entered. These major collections wil be supplemented by the addition of economic information from the wills, probate records, and tax records. Additional vital statistics will be added from church records, partial census returns, Loyalist Claims Commission petitions and military records. Altogether these records should give some information on almost all the inhabitants of the province in this period, and quite a bit of information on particular inhabitants, hopefully, a high proportion of them.

To give some idea of the size of the records with which I am dealing here is a list of those that we have coded, or are coding, to date.

	Heads of Households	Number of Variables
RG 1 — E.C. Wright List	6,131	20
RG 2 — 1783 Census	176	21
RG 3 — Land Grants & Cadestral Maps	9,309	29
RG 4 — Partial Census 1785	398	16
RG 5 — Partial Census 1803	126	13
RG 6 — Loyalist Register	3,785	20
RG 7 — Land Petitions	11,000	40

As examples of the kinds of detail contained on the records, here are lists of the variables from two of the land records.

RG 3 — Land Grants and Cadestrals.
   —name of grantee
   —exact location of grant (modern bearings of latitude and longitude, parish and county location)
   —occupation of grantee
   —number of acres in grant
   —date of grant
   —names of co-grantees, if a group grant.

RG 7 — Land Petitions
   —name of petitioner
   —date of petition
   —Group identity (Revolutionary War Service, or "Loyalist exile" or Acadian or Early-English, etc.)
   —occupation
   —origin
   —location of land by name and county
   —improvements
   —family size
   —marital status
   —education of petitioner
   —size of grant requested

The data that I am using in the New Brunswick study also exist for 'Loyalist' societies established elsewhere in British North America. This includes such societies in Ontario, Prince Edward Island, Cape Breton Island, Nova Scotia and Quebec, although the final two areas have their Loyalist records obscured to some extent by the existence of, in the case of Nova Scotia, an equal "Pre-Loyalist" population, and in Quebec, by a preponderant population of French-Canadians. It would seem most fruitful to concentrate attention, in the first instance, on those areas where Loyalist settlers made up almost the entire population. These areas are the provinces of New Brunswick and Ontario.

Likewise, there are lists of Loyalists for other areas in Canada equivalent to the Wright Loyalist list in New Brunswick. Nova Scotia loyalists are listed in Marion Gilroy's *Loyalists and Land Settlement in Nova Scotia.*[8] Cape Breton and Prince Edward Island lists are available in manuscript. Ontario is probably the best documented area of Loyalist settlement with two published lists of Loyalists and information about them. First, there is the so-called U.E. List preserved in the Crown Lands Department at Toronto which was published in 1885 as an appendix to a book documenting the centennial celebrations of the settlement of Upper Canada.[9] This list contains about 5,000 names of heads of families, along with place of residence, military service, marital state, number of children, and other miscellaneous information. *The Loyalists in Ontario,*[10] published in 1973, is a list of the sons and daughters of the Upper Canada Loyalists. It was compiled over many years by William D. Reid, an employee of the Ontario Archives. The information was extracted from Orders-In-Council as land was granted to the children of the Loyalists. It lists the name of the Loyalist, the name of his wife, the date of marriage, the names of their children, along with birth dates, the names of the children's spouses and, in many cases, death dates for members of the family. The list contains some 2,500 households.

There are other lists of Canadian Loyalists also available. The obsession of genealogists with this period has provided the incentive for the production of these lists. For example, the Public Archives of Canada staff has abstracted lists of Loyalists from large collections such as the Haldimand Papers. The various provincial archives maintain extensive nominal files for this period. Additionally, the U.E.L. Association of Canada requires a genealogy illustrating a potential member's U.E.L. ancestry. A copy of each genealogy is put on file in the Toronto office. Although I do not envisage using it in my own work, this large amount of genealogical material on Canadian Loyalists should be considered by anyone undertaking quantitative research in this period. This material has to be viewed as secondary, but with careful checking it should be possible to use it as an additional source for family reconstitution studies.

It has been customary over the past few years at conferences such as this one to lament the scholarly neglect of the Loyalists. I do not feel, in terms of Canadian Scholarship at least, that this complaint can continue to be made. A good deal of interest in Loyalists studies has developed over the past five years in Canada, due at least in part to the work of the Loyalist Studies Programme.[11] Any area of history can always benefit from increased attention by scholars, but Loyalist studies are now, in my opinion, receiving at least a fair share of attention from Canadian historians. Most of the work completed or under way on the Loyalists in Canada deals with them from the traditional approaches of political or ideological history, with a few excursions into social history. I expect that we will see research on the Loyalists go in new directions over the next few years. It strikes me as an appropriate time to establish some basic demographic facts about the Loyalists, and about the societies that they established or helped to establish in Canada. The means, both of sources and methods, exist to establish the "facts of life" about such societies: population size, age distributions, marital conditions, size of families, birth and death rates, and number of children. Furthermore, the facts of land settlement and community and regional development are determinable.

Given the facts, the variety of interpretive work possible is limited only by the ingenuity of the individual researcher. A list of theories ranging from the long-established, such as the Frontier or Laurentian theories, to the relatively new interpretations such as the Hartzean ideas on social development can be illustrated and tested. Additionally, I expect that as the demographic, social and economic facts are detailed and examined, new interpretations can be developed. The fact that, in this instance, one is dealing with societies established by the Loyalists of the American Revolution simply adds an additional richness to the possible interpretations. It will be very interesting, for example, to discover how, or if, societies composed of "Loyalist" Americans differ from those maintained by "Patriot" Americans in the United States, and whether their future developments vary or parallel each other. I expect, therefore, that quantitatively-oriented research on the Loyalists in Canada will prove a fruitful area of study.

Overall, the possibilities for research in demography, social structure and land settlement appear very promising in the Loyalist-dominated era of Canadian history. The data certainly exist for such studies. There is also the possibility of linking up with similar studies undertaken on the Loyalists before they left the United States. Furthermore, there is the possibility of comparing the results of such studies with the findings of demographic studies on societies and communities in the United States, Great Britain and Europe in the second half of the eighteenth century, and the early part of the nineteenth.

1. Leonard W. Labaree, *Conservatism in Early American History* (New York, 1948), pp. 165-66.
2. William H. Nelson, *The American Tory* (Oxford, 1961), p. 188.
3. Bernard Bailyn, *The Ordeal of Thomas Hutchinson* (Cambridge, Mass., 1974), p. 378.
4. Carl Berger, *The Sense of Power: Studies in the Ideas of Canadian Imperialism, 1867-1914* (Toronto, 1970), pp. 78-108.
5. Bailyn, *op. cit.,* pp. 396-401.
6. Sewall has been the subject of one full-length biography, Carol Berkin's *Jonathan Sewall, a Loyalist Odyssey* (New York, 1974), and two biographical essays: Robert M. Calhoon, *The Loyalists in Revolutionary America, 1760-1781* (New York, 1973), pp. 68-75 and Clifford K. Shipton, *Sibley's Harvard Graduates* (Boston, 1933-74), XII, 306-325. The factual material in the following paragraphs is drawn from these accounts.
7. John Adams, *The Diary and Autobiography of John Adams,* Lyman H. Butterfield, *et. al.,* eds. (Cambridge, Mass., 1961), III, 278.
8. Edward Winslow to Jonathan Sewall, jr., 1 November 1790, Sewall Correspondence (Public Archives of Canada).
9. Adams, *Diary,* I, 375.
10. Jonathan Sewall to Judge Joseph Lee, 21 September 1787, Lee Family Papers (Massachusetts Historical Society).
11. The opinion is printed in Oliver M. Dickerson, "Opinion of Attorney General Sewall of Massachusetts in the Case of the *Lydia," William and Mary Quarterly,* 3rd Series, 4 (1947), 500-504.
12. For this interpretation of Sewall's conduct, I am indebted to Berkin, *Jonathan Sewall,* pp. 83-86.
13. Sewall wrote four series of essays between 1763 and 1775 under different pseudonyms. They were:

a. Letters from "J," *Boston Evening Post,* February 14, March 14, March 28, April 4, April 25, May 23 Supplement, and June 13, 1763.

b. Letters from "Philanthrop," *Boston Evening Post,* December 1, December 15, and December 29, 1766; January 4, January 12, January 26, February 9, March 2, July 27, August 3, and August 10, 1767.

c. Letters from "Philanthrop," *Boston Evening Post,* December 24, 1770; January 14, January 28, February 4, and February 18, 1771.

d. Letters from "Philalethes," *Massachusetts Gazette and Boston Weekly Newsletter,* June 17, June 24, July 1, July 15, July 22, August 5, and August 12, 1773.

14. Letter from "Philanthrop," *Boston Evening Post,* January 14, 1771.
15. *Ibid.,* December 1, 1766.
16. "Letters of Jonathan Sewall," *Proceedings of the Massachusetts Historical Society,* Second series, 10 (1895, 1896), 407.
17. Letter from "J," *Boston Evening Post,* May 23, 1763 Supplement.
18. *Ibid.*
19. *Ibid.,* April 25, 1763.
20. *Ibid.,* May 14, 1763.
21. Letter from "Philanthrop," *Boston Evening Post,* January 14, 1771.
22. *Ibid.,* January 26, 1767.
23. *Ibid.,* December 1, 1766.
24. *Ibid.,* January 14 and February 4, 1771.
25. *Ibid.,* December 24, 1770.
26. *Ibid.,* January 26, 27. *Ibid.,* January 14, 1771.
28. Letter from "Philalethes," *Massachusetts Gazette,* June 24, 1773.
29. "Letters of Jonathan Sewall," *MHS Proceedings,* p. 413.
30. Quoted by Shipton, *Sibley's Harvard Graduates,* XII, 319

31. Jonathan Sewall to Ward Chipman, 20 April 1782, Lawrence Collection, Chipman Papers (Public Archives of Canada).
32. Jonathan Sewall to Ward Chipman, 23 March 1782, Lawrence Collection.
33. Jonathan Sewall to Edward Winslow, 20 September 1778, Winslow Papers (University of New Brunswick).
34. Jonathan Sewall to Ward Chipman, 23 March 1782, Lawrence Collection.
35. Jonathan Sewall to Ward Chipman, 1 February 1783, Lawrence Collection.
36. Jonathan Sewall to Ward Chipman, 17 April 1782, Sewall Correspondence.
37. Sewall's plan is published in Julian P. Boyd, *Anglo-American Union: Joseph Galloway's Plans to Preserve the British Empire, 1774–1788* (Philadelphia, 1941), pp. 157-72. William H. Nelson presents conclusive evidence attributing the authorship of this plan to Sewall rather than Galloway, in "Last Hopes of the American Loyalists," *Canadian Historical Review*, 32 (1951), 40-42.
38. Nelson, "Last Hopes," p. 40.

NOTES TO JENNINGS

1. Samuel Purchas, *Hakluytus Posthumus or Purchas His Pilgrimes*, 4, vols. (London, 1625), IV, 1811, 1814.
2. *The Papers of Sir William Johnson*, edited by James Sullivan *et. al.*, 14 vols. (Albany, 1921–1965), XII, 994-995.
3. *Ibid.*, XI, 925.
4. Thomas Perkins Abernethy, *Western Lands and the American Revolution* (1937, reprinted N.Y., 1959), ch. 6; Gwenda Morgan, "Virginia and the French and Indian War: A Case Study of the War's Effects on Imperial Relations," *Virginia Magazine of History and Biography*, 81 (1973), 36-38.

5. Forbes to Bouquet, 9 August 1758, in *Writings of General John Forbes Relating to His Service in North America* (Menasha, Wis., 1938), 171.

6. C.A. Weslager, *The Delaware Indians: A History* (New Brunswick, N.J., 1972), 286; Anthony F.C. Wallace, *The Death and Rebirth of the Seneca* (New York, 1970), 122.

7. The best history is Howard H. Peckham, *Pontiac and the Indian Uprising* (1947, reprinted Chicago, 1961).

8. *Ibid.,* 170. This fact was challenged by Bernhard Knollenberg who listed the source documents and interpreted them so as to excuse Amherst, but the challenge drew forth a counter-challenger who produced new evidence so conclusive that Knollenberg conceded. See Bernhard Knollenberg, "General Amherst and Germ Warfare," *Mississippi Valley Historical Review,* 41 (Dec. 1954), 489-494; and the additional evidence provided by Donald H. Kent, together with Knollenberg's retraction, in "Communications," *ibid.,* 41 (March 1955), 762-763.

9. Jack M. Sosin, *Whitehall and the Wilderness: The Middle West in British Colonial Policy, 1760–1775* (Lincoln, Neb., 1961), chs. 4, 5.

10. Lawrence Henry Gipson, *The British Empire Before the American Revolution,* 15 vols. (New York, 1939-1970), V, 107-112.

11. The Plan of Union is in *Documents Relating to the Colonial History of the State of New York,* edited by Edmund B. O'Callaghan and Berthold Fernow, 15 vols. (Albany, 1856–1887), VI, 889-891. Its rejection is discussed in Gipson, *British Empire,* V, ch. 5. The varied origins of the Superintendency are in John R. Alden, "The Albany Congress and the Creation of the Indian Superintendencies," *Mississippi Valley Historical Review,* 27 (Sep. 1940), 193-210; and *The Appalachian Indian Frontier: The Edmond Atkin Report and Plan of 1755,* edited by Wilbur R. Jacobs (1954, reprinted Lincoln, Neb., 1967).

12. The Proclamation (with many associated documents) is in *Documents Relating to the Constitutional History of Canada, 1759–1791,* edited by Adam Shortt and Arthur G.

Doughty, *Canadian Archives Sessional Paper No. 18* (Ottawa, 1907), 119-123.

13. Abernethy, *Western Lands,* 8.

14. *Ibid.,* chs. 2-10; Sosin, *Whitehall and the Wilderness,* chs. 6-9.

15. Shortt and Doughty, eds., *Documents . . . of Canada,* 433-437; Sosin, *Whitehall and the Wilderness,* 73-77.

16. Jack M. Sosin, *The Revolutionary Frontier, 1763-1783* (New York, 1967), chs. 3, 4.

17. Shortt and Doughty, eds., *Documents . . . of Canada,* 401-405, 428.

18. Sosin, *Whitehall and the Wilderness,* ch. 10, esp. p. 245.

19. Gustave Lanctot, *Canada and the American Revolution, 1774-1783* (Cambridge, Mass., 1967), chs. 2-10. It is especially noteworthy that before the Quebec Act the Virginia gentry had tacitly accepted the crown's power to change colonial boundaries. Upon the Act's passage, however, Thomas Jefferson wrote *A Summary View of the Rights of British America* in which he denounced "the fictitious principle that all lands belong originally to the king" and claimed that "all the lands within the limits which any particular society *has circumscribed around itself* are assumed by that society [read, "Virginia"] and subject to their allotment only." Abernethy, *Western Lands,* 129, 148; *Tracts of the American Revolution, 1763-1776,* edited by Merrill Jensen (Indianapolis, 1967), 273. Emphasis added.

20. Barbara Graymont, *The Iroquois in the American Revolution* (Syracuse, N.Y., 1972), chs. 4, 5. The variant pattern in the southern region is discussed in James H. O'Donnell, III, *Southern Indians in the American Revolution* (Knoxville, Tenn., 1973).

21. Graymont, *Iroquois in the American Revolution,* ch. 10; A.F.C. Wallace, *Death and Rebirth of the Seneca,* 149-152.

22. Graymont, *Iroquois in the American Revolution,* 282-283; Donald H. Kent, *History of Pennsylvania Purchases from the Indians,* The Garland American Indian Ethnohistory Series: Iroquois Indians, I (New York, 1974), 83-115, 124. The curious discrepancy between the policies of Pennsylvania and the United States is highlighted by Penn-

sylvania's further procedure in purchasing the claims of the Wyandot and Delaware Indians in 1785. Under the conquest theory this act was doubly unnecessary: (1) because all the Indians supposedly stood in the status of conquered peoples; (2) because the lands in question had supposedly been at the disposal of the Iroquois Six Nations instead of these formerly tributory tribes. *Minutes of the Second Session of the Ninth General Assembly of the Commonwealth of Pennsylvania,* Appendix, 314-328; Minutes of the Proceedings at Fort McIntosh, 9-21 January 1785, Wayne MSS., Indian Treaties, B.

Extracts from Journal of the Commissioners of Indian Affairs for the Northern and Middle Departments, 57-59. Historical Society of Pennsylvania, Philadelphia, Pa.

23. Wilcomb E. Washburn, *Red Man's Land/White Man's Law: A Study of the Past and Present Status of the American Indian* (New York, 1971), 54-58; 73; 109-123.

NOTES TO MARSHALL

1. Jack M. Sosin, "The Use of Indians in the War of the American Revolution: A Re-Assessment of Responsibility," *Canadian Historical Review,* XLVI (1965), 121.
2. Wallace Brown, *The King's Friends* (Providence, R.I., 1966), p. 106. Mary Beth Norton, "Eardley-Wilmot, Britannia, and the Loyalists: A Painting by Benjamin West," *Perspectives in American History,* VI (1972), 119-131.
3. Brown, *op.cit.,* pp. 276-277.
4. Robert McCluer Calhoon, *The Loyalists in Revolutionary America 1760–1781* (New York, 1973), p. 424.
5. James H. O'Donnell III, *Southern Indians in the American Revolution* (Knoxville, Tenn., 1973), p. 141.

6. *Ibid.,* p. 143. Another recent account has calculated the steady growth in the cost of Indian presents dispatched from Britain. A total in 1775 of £2,541 19s 10d had swollen by 1782 to £63,861 17s 7d, it being observed of the destination that: "In the early years of the war there was a reasonably even balance between the volume of presents sent to Canada and those sent to the southern department. In the later stages of the war the volume of goods sent to Canada represented an increasingly high proportion of the whole." Norman, Baker, *Government and Contractors* (London, 1971), p. 200.

7. Tonyn to Carleton, 23 Dec. 1782, *HMC Report on American Manuscripts in the Royal Institution of Great Britain* (Hereford, 1907), III. 276-277.
   23 Dec. 1782, "Return of Loyalists," *ibid.,* p. 276.

8. Charles Loch Mowat, *East Florida as a British Province 1763-1784* (Berkeley & Los Angeles, 1943), pp. 138-142.

9. Brown to Carleton, 28 Apr. 1783, *Report on American Manuscripts . . .* IV.59.

10. McArthur to Carleton, 19 May 1783, *ibid.,* IV.89.

11. Brown to Carleton, 1 June 1783, *ibid.,* IV.119.

12. Carleton to McArthur, 19 June 1783, *ibid.,* IV.165.

13. McArthur to Carleton, 12 Sept. 1783, 19 July 1783, *ibid.,* IV. 351, 233.

14. Wilbur Henry Siebert, *Loyalists in East Florida, 1774 to 1785 . . .* (Boston, 1972), I.148.

15. McGillivray to Miro, 28 Mar. 1784, John Walton Caughey, *McGillivray of the Creeks* (Norman, Okla., 1959), pp. 73-74.

16. O'Donnell, *op.cit.,* p. 12.

17. A.L. Burt, *The Old Province of Quebec* (Toronto, 1968), II. 56. Maclean to Haldimand, 18 May 1783, Charles M. Johnston *ed., The Valley of the Six Nations* (Toronto, 1964), pp. 35-36.

18. Speech of Brant to Haldimand at Quebec, 21 May 1783, Johnston, *op.cit.,* pp. 49-51.

19. George F.G. Stanley, "The Six Nations and the American Revolution," *Ontario History,* LVI (1964), 225.

20. Barbara Graymont, *The Iroquois in the American Revolution* (Syracuse, N.Y., 1972), p. 66.
21. Wilbur H. Siebert, "The Loyalists and Six Nation Indians in the Niagara Peninsula," *Transactions* of the Royal Society of Canada, Third Series, IX (1915), 80.
22. William L. Stone, *Life of Joseph Brant* (New York, 1838), I. 89-90. Brant gave these details in a speech delivered in 1803. Since he gave the month of the meeting as July and declared the speech to have been by Haldimand, the accuracy of the report must remain doubtful. Brant's claim closely resembles the general tenor of Loyalist evidence.
23. Brant to Sir John Johnson, Nov. 1801, *ibid.,* II. 408.
24. *Ibid.,* II. 402-404. Siebert, *loc.cit.,* p. 93.
25. Graymont, *op.cit.,* pp. 142, 192.
26. *Ibid.,* pp. 240-241.
27. Gary D. Olson, "Thomas Brown, Partisan, and the Revolutionary War in Georgia, 1777–1782," *Georgia Historical Quarterly,* LIV (1970), 196-197. Robert F. Berkhofer, Jr., "Barrier to Settlement: British Indian Policy in the Old Northwest, 1783–1794," *The Frontier in American Development,* David M. Ellis *ed.,* (Ithaca, N.Y., 1969), pp. 250-251.
28. Quoted Berkhofer, *loc. cit.,* p. 253.
29. North to Haldimand, 8 Aug. 1783, Johnson, *op.cit.,* p. 42.
30. Reginald Horsman, *Expansion and American Indian Policy, 1783–1812* (East Lansing, Mich., 1967), pp. 4-15.
31. Quoted Berkhofer, *loc.cit.,* p. 253.
32. Anthony F.C. Wallace, *The Death and Rebirth of the Seneca* (New York, 1972), pp. 144-146.
33. Berkhofer, *loc.cit.,* pp. 255-256.
34. On the making of the 1768 boundary, see my article, "Sir William Johnson and the Treaty of Fort Stanwix," *Journal of American Studies,* I (1967), 149-179.
35. Graymont, *op.cit.,* pp. 232, 158-159.
36. "Substance of Brant's Wishes Respecting Forming a Settlement on the Grand River," and Haldimand's Answer, March 1783. Johnson, *op.cit.,* pp. 44-45. The date should read March 1784.

37. Haldimand's Proclamation of 25 Oct. 1784. Robert Matthews to John Stuart, 30 Oct. 1784. Sale of Grand River Lands to the Crown, 22 May 1784. Johnston, *op.cit.*, pp. 50-51, 48. Siebert, *loc.cit.*, p. 118.

38. Sydney to Haldimand, 8 Apr. 1784, Johnston, *op.cit.*, pp. 45-46.

39. Patrick Campbell, *Travels in North America* (Toronto, 1937), p. 178.

40. Census, Johnston, *op.cit.*, p. 52.

41. Brown, *op.cit.*, p. 277. The Crown Lands Department at Toronto "Old U.E. List" notes four sons and three daughters of Sir William Johnson and Mary Brant as recipients of land. The Supplementary list adds Sally Ainise, 'A principal Indian woman,' John Deserontyo, a Mohawk chief, and Aaron and Isaac Hill, similarly described. United Empire Loyalist Centennial Committee, *The Centennial of the Settlement of Upper Canada* . . . (Boston, 1972), pp. 198-199, 283, 301.

42. Graymont, *op.cit.*, p. 285.

43. Stone, *op.cit.*, II. 398. F. Klinck and James J. Talman *eds.*, *The Journal of Major John Norton 1816* (Toronto, 1970), pp. 270-271, 284-285.

44. Campbell, *op.cit.*, pp. 165, 167.

45. Horsman, *op.cit.*, p. 17.

46. *Ibid.*, pp. 17-19. Graymont, *op.cit.*, pp. 297-298. Wallace, *op.cit.*, pp. 151-152.

47. Graymont, *op.cit.*, pp. 287-288.

48. Wallace, *op.cit.*, pp. 167-168.

49. Peter A. Cumming and Neil H. Mickenberg *eds.*, *Native Rights in Canada* (2nd ed., Toronto, 1972), p. 30.

50. Proclamation of 7 Oct. 1763, C.W. Alvord and C.E. Carter *eds.*, *The Critical Period 1763–1765, Collections* of the Illinois State Historical Library, X.44.

51. Brant to James Green, 10 Dec. 1797, Johnston, *op.cit.*, p. 92.

52. Stone, *op.cit.*, II. 403.

53. Cumming and Mickenberg, *op.cit.*, p. 111. C.M. Johnston, *Brant County. A History 1784–1945* (Toronto, 1967), pp. 102-104.

54. Graymont, *op.cit.*, pp. 292-294. Doubt is expressed on this point by Lillian F. Gates, *Land Policies of Upper Canada* (Toronto, 1968), p. 49.
55. William Johnson Kerr to John Macaulay, 3 October 1838, Johnston, *Valley of the Six Nations,* pp. 230-231.
56. Malcolm Montgomery, "The Legal Status of the Six Nations Indians in Canada," *Ontario History,* LV (1963), pp. 96-97.
57. *Ibid.,* p. 93.
58. *Ibid.,* p. 100.
59. Samuel Flagg Bemis, *Jay's Treaty* (New Haven, 1962), p. 457.
60. Montgomery, *loc.cit.,* pp. 95-96. Cumming and Mickenberg, *op.cit.,* p. 55.
61. Montgomery, *loc.cit.,* p. 103.

NOTES TO RAWLYK

1. J. Strachan, *A Sermon on the Death of the Rev. John Stuart D.D.* (Kingston, 1811), p. 29.
2. Charles Inglis to Sir W. Johnson, Sept. 21, 1771, in E.B. O'Callaghan (ed.), *Documentary History of the State of New York* (Albany, 1851), Vol. IV, p. 289.
3. Quoted in J.W. Lydekker, "The Reverend John Stuart, D.D. (1740–1811), Missionary to the Mohawks," *Historical Magazine of the Protestant Episcopal Church,* Vol. X (March, 1942), pp. 62-63.
4. Quoted in *ibid.,* p. 61.
5. J. Strachan, "Memoir of the Reverend John Stuart, D.D.," in O'Callaghan, *Documentary History of the State of New York,* Vol. IV, p. 321; Strachan, *A Sermon,* p. 22.
6. Strachan, *A Sermon,* p. 22.
7. Quoted in Lydekker, "The Reverend John Stuart," p. 63.
8. The biographical sketch is based upon Strachan's "Memoir," pp. 314-315 and on Strachan *A Sermon,* pp. 23-25. Very valuable information about Stuart's New York during the

Revolutionary years is to be found in B. Graymont, *The Iroquois in the American Revolution* (Syracuse, 1972), S.F. Wise "The Northern Indians in the American Revolution," (Unpublished M.A. Thesis, Queen's University, 1952) and in R.J. Ashton, "The Loyalist Experience: New York, 1763-1789; (Unpublished Ph.D. Dissertation, Northeastern University, 1973). Useful background material concerning the formative period of Upper Canada's history may be found in G.H. Craig, *Upper Canada: The Formative Years, 1784-1841* (Toronto, 1963) and about Kingston in R. Preston's long introduction to *Kingston Before the War of 1812* (Toronto, 1959).

9. Smith to Johnson, March 31, 1770, in A. Flick (ed.), *The Papers of Sir William Johnson* (Albany, 1931) Vol. VII, pp. 517-518.
10. Johnson to Richard Peters, William Smith and Thomas Barton, April 16, 1770, in *ibid., p.* 566.
11. Inglis to S.P.G., June 15, 1770, in J.W. Lydekker, *The Faithful Mohawks* (Cambridge, 1938), pp. 124-125.
12. Inglis to S.P.G., March 8, 1770, Journals of the S.P.G. (Microfilm).
13. Barton to Johnson, July 26, 1770, in Flick, *Johnson Papers,* Vol. VII. p. 811.
14. *Ibid.*
15. Johnson to Inglis, Nov. 1770, in O'Callaghan, *Documentary History,* Vol. IV, p. 268.
16. Johnson to Barton, Feb. 28, 1771, in *ibid,* p. 274.
17. Lydekker, "The Reverend John Stuart," p. 21.
18. Stuart to S.P.G., Jan. 8, 1772, in *ibid,* p. 23.
19. Inglis to S.P.G., in J.W. Lydekker, *The Life and Letters of Charles Inglis* (London, 1936) pp. 124-125. See also Johnson to Inglis, March 27, 1771, in O'Callaghan, *Documentary History,* Vol. IV, p. 277.
20. Stuart to S.P.G., June 22, 1771, in Lydekker, "The Reverend John Stuart," p. 22; Stuart to S.P.G., July 20, 1772, *ibid.,* p. 25.
21. Stuart to S.P.G., July 20, 1772, in *ibid.,* p. 25.
22. Stuart to S.P.G., August 9, 1774, in *ibid.,* p. 29.

23. Stuart to S.P.G., July 20, 1772, in *ibid.*, pp. 26-27.
24. Stuart to S.P.G., Feb. 13, 1774, in *ibid.*, p. 27.
25. Stuart to S.P.G., Aug. 9, 1774, in *ibid.*, p. 30.
26. *Ibid.*
27. Strachan, *A Sermon*, p. 28.
28. J.B. Robinson's view as quoted in *ibid.*, p. 64.
29. Stuart to White, June 17, 1785, Public Archives of Ontario (P.A.O.), White Papers.
30. Lydekker, "The Reverend John Stuart," p. 60.
31. Quoted in B. Graymont, *The Iroquois in the American Revolution* (Syracuse, 1972) p. 63.
32. *Ibid.*, pp. 63-64.
33. E.B. O'Callaghan (ed.), *Documents Relative to the Colonial History of the State of New York* (Albany, 1857) Vol. VIII, pp. 623, 625.
34. Stuart to S.P.G., October 27, 1775, in Lydekker, "The Reverend John Stuart," p. 34.
35. Strachan, "Memoir," p. 315.
36. *Ibid.*
37. Quoted in *ibid.*, pp. 315-316.
38. Stuart to S.P.G. Oct. 13, 1781, in Lydekker, "The Reverend John Stuart," p. 40.
39. Minutes of the Commissioners In Detecting Conspiracies, I, pp. 69., 87-8, quoted in Strachan, "Memoir," p. 315.
40. *Ibid.*, pp. 315-316.
41. Stuart to White, Sept. 28, 1778, P.A.O. White Papers.
42. *Ibid.*
43. Minutes of the Commissioners In Detecting Conspiracies, June 28, 1779, quoted in Strachan, "Memoir," p. 316.
44. *Ibid.*
45. Stuart to White, June 12, 1780, P.A.O., White Papers.
46. Strachan, "Memoir," p. 316.
47. Quoted in *ibid.*, p. 316.
48. Stuart to White, November 13, 1780, P.A.O., White Papers.
49. *Ibid.*
50. Stuart to J.B. Robinson, April 23, 1805, P.A.O. J.B. Robinson Papers.
51. Stuart to White, April 19, 1781, P.A.O., White Papers.

52. Stuart to White, Sept. 16, 1781, P.A.O., White Papers.
53. Stuart to White, Nov. 2, 1785, P.A.O., White Papers.
54. Stuart to White, Sept. 4, 1788, P.A.O., White Papers.
55. Stuart to White, Nov. 26, 1798, P.A.O., White Papers.
56. Stuart to White, Sept. 4, 1788, P.A.O., White Papers.
57. Stuart to White, Jan. 7, 1798, P.A.O., White Papers.
58. *Kingston Gazette,* Aug. 20, 1811.

NOTES TO BROWN

1. Elizabeth L. Johnston, *Recollections of a Georgia Loyalist,* ed. Arthur W. Eaton (New York and London, 1901) p. 211.
2. *Ibid.,* p. 215.
3. Siebert Papers, p. 12, Box 35, The Ohio Historical Society, Columbus, Ohio. Microfilm copies used.
4. August 24, 1782.
5. William Dwarris to L. Smith, April 6, 1783, William Dwarris Letters, West India Committee, London.
6. *The Cornwall Chronicle,* March 8, 1783. This rare paper may be consulted in the Bristol Public Library.
7. William Dwarris to L. Smith, April 6, 1783, Dwarris Letters.
8. C071/8, ff. 212-213 (Colonial Office Papers), Public Record Office, London.
9. Journal of the Council, October 29, 1782, Archives, Spanish Town, Jamaica.
10. C071/8, ff. 212-214; Thelma Peters, *The American Loyalists and the Plantation Period in the Bahama Islands,* Ph.D. diss., The University of Florida, 1960, p. 68.
11. *Journals of the Assembly of Jamaica, 1663–1826* (Kingston, Jamaica, 1803–1826), VIII, 148-149.
12. C071/9, ff. 193-198, 213, 218-219; Thomas Rainey to Lieut. Col. William Myers, September 27, 1791, C071/21.
13. C071/13; C071/8, f. 310.

14. Peters, *The American Loyalists,* p. 172.
15. *Ibid.,* p. 27.
16. Clifford H. Shipton, *Sibley's Harvard Graduates: Biographical Sketches of Those Who Attended Harvard College* (Boston, 1951), XIII, 485.
17. William Wylly, *A Short Account of the Bahama Islands, their Climate, Productions &c,* 1788, p. 9, Add. mss 6058, British Museum, London. This manuscript was published in London in 1789.
18. W.H. Seibert, *Loyalists in East Florida, 1774 to 1785,* (Deland, Florida, 1929), I, 205; George W. Roberts, *The Population of Jamaica* (Cambridge, 1957), p. 29.
19. September 6, 1787, C071/13; C023/25 f. 381.
20. Amos K. Fiske, *The West Indies* (New York, 1899), pp. 116-117.
21. Michael Craton, *A History of the Bahamas* (London, 1968), p. 105; Siebert, *Loyalists in East Florida,* I, 204.
22. Historical Manuscript Commission, *Report on American Manuscripts in the Royal Institution,* III, 45; Wallace Brown, *The Good Americans* (New York, 1969), p. 214.
23. North Callahan, *Flight From the Republic* (Indianapolis, 1967), p. 100; Peters, *The American Loyalists,* p. 163.
24. *Ibid.,* pp. 49-51, 33-34; Nathaniel Hall to William Gibbons, Jr., November 1, 1789, #449, Telfair Family Papers, Georgia Historical Society, Savannah, Georgia.
25. Peters, *The American Loyalists,* pp. 148-150; Wylly, *A Short Account,* p. 7; Alan Burns, *History of the British West Indies* (London, 1954), p. 536.
26. The Reverend Philip Dixon to Dr. Morice, August 10, 1802. Bahamas, Box 2, 1790–1810, The United Society for the Propagation of the Gospel, London.
27. Peters, *The American Loyalists, pp. 188, 163 and passim* Ch. VI.
28. Journal of the House of Assembly, November 25, 1802, Mss in the Public Archives, Nassau; Peters, *The American Loyalists,* pp. 76-77, 158-159; Mathew B. Hammond, *The Cotton Industry: An Essay in American Economic History* (New York, 1897), pp. 16-17.

29. Peters, *The American Loyalists, p. 167.*

30. *Caleb Dickinson to Bryan Edwards, September 23, 1799, C107/68 (Chancery Papers), PRO, London.*

31. *Henry Rugeley to his mother, October 2, 1784, Henry Rugeley to Mathew Rugeley, July 28, 1784, Henry Rugeley Letters, 1783-1790, Bedford County Record Office.*

32. *Johnston, Recollections, p. 218.*

33. Memorial, August 1, 1783, C0137/72.

34. Frank Cundall, *Chronological Outline of Jamaica History* (Kingston, 1927), p. 24.

35. Edward Braithwaite, *The Development of Creole Society in Jamaica, 1770-1820* (Oxford, 1971), p. 84.

36. Thomas Southey, *Chronological History of the West Indies* (London, 1827, II, 542.

37. George W. Bridges, *The Annals of Jamaica* (London, 1828), I, 507.

38. Lydia A. Parrish, *Records of Some Southern Loyalists, p. 7,* Ms., Houghton Library, Harvard University.

39. Peters, *The American Loyalists,* pp. 119-124; 131; George Barry to ?, June 30, 1786, CO23/26.

40. November 27, 1787, C023/27.

41. J.D. Schoepf, *Travels in the Confederation, 1783-4,* (Philadelphia, 1911); Daniel McKinnon, *A Tour Through the British West Indies in the Years 1802 and 1803,* (London, 1804); *A Relic of Slavery: Farquharson's Journal for 1833-32,* (Nassau, 1957).

42. Parrish, *Records,* p. 49; Peters, *The American Loyalists,* pp. 135, 137, 141; William Dwarris to Lilley Smith, April 22, 1788, Dwarris Letters.

43. *The Cornwall Chronicle,* January 18, 1783; C0101/8 ff. 374-75; Peters, *The American Loyalists, p. 45.*

44. A.B. Ellis, *The History of the First West India Regiment* (London, 1885), p. 51.

45. Lawrence Kinnaird, "International Rivalry in the Creek Country," *Florida Historical Quarterly,* X (October, 1931), pp. 59-85; Peters, *The American Loyalists,* pp. 103-119.

46. Craton, *History of the Bahamas,* p. 164; Peters, *The American Loyalists,* p. 82; Brown, *Good Americans,* p. 221.

47. Peters, *The American Loyalists,* p. 51; Richard Kent, ed., *Letters from the Bahama Islands Written in 1823-4* (London, 1948), p. 43.
48. *S. P. G. Reports* for 1792 and 1793, the United Society for the Progagation of the Gospel, London.
49. Journal of the House of Assembly, June 25, 1790; Peters, The American Loyalists, p. 172.
50. *Ibid.,* pp. 95, 99.
51. *Ibid.,* 88-89; Miscellaneous Papers, C023/26; C023/25 f. 179. For the whole political quarrel in the Bahamas see Peters, The American Loyalists, ch. IV, Craton, *History of the Bahamas,* chs. XII, XV, XVI, and C023/15, 25, 27, 28.
52. Craton, *History of the Bahamas,* pp. 168-170.
53. Peters, *The American Loyalists,* p. 93.
54. Burns, *History of the British West Indies,* p. 544.
55. C0137/85, f. 154.
56. *Journals of the Assembly of Jamaica,* VIII, 136, 126; Kingston Vestry Proceedings, Mss in the Archives, Spanish Town, November, 1784.
57. *Journals of the Assembly of Jamaica,* VIII, 148; Johnston, *Recollections,* p. 85.
58. Henry Rugeley to his mother, February 28, 1783, Henry Rugeley Letters.
59. Frank Cundall, *History of Printing in Jamaica* (Kingston, 1935), pp. 32-33; Siebert, *Loyalists in East Florida,* I, 205; Louisa S. Wells, *The Journal of a Voyage from Charlestown to London* (New York, 1968), pp. 108, 111-112.
60. Cundall, *History of Printing,* pp. 14-17, 33.
61. Craton, *History of the Bahamas,* p. 305; Siebert, *Loyalists in East Florida,* I, 134-135, 189.
62. Peters, *The American Loyalists,* pp. 160-162.
63. *Ibid.,* pp. 79, 24.
64. *Ibid.,* p. 81.
65. Schoepf, *Travels in the Confederation,* p. 262; Peters, *The American Loyalists,* p. 48.
66. *Ibid.,* pp. 169, 176-177, 181.
67. *Jamaica Almanack* (1785), p. 64.
68. Sketch of a Plan . . . (undated), C0260/7; Peters, *The American Loyalists,* pp. 58 ff.

69. C071/9 f. 213; John Robinson to Thomas Orde, July 1, 1791, Melville Castle Muniments, Scottish Record Office, Edinburgh.
70. Lennox Honeychurch to the author, July 30, 1975.
71. Bridges, *Annals of Jamaica,* I, 195.
72. Lowell J. Ragatz, *A Guide for the Study of British Caribbean History* (Washington, D.C., 1932), p. iii.
73. A. Talbot Bethell, *The Early Settlers of the Bahamas and Colonists of North America* (Nassau, 1937), p. 125.
74. Reported in the *Royal Gazette,* Hamilton, Bermuda, July 9, 1973.
75. Peters, *The American Loyalists,* p. 186.
76. Kent, ed., *Letters from the Bahama Islands,* p. 40.
77. Peters, *The American Loyalists,* p. 187.
78. Paul Albury, *The Story of the Bahamas,* (London, 1975).

NOTES TO WRIGHT

1. Bruere to the Earl of Dartmouth, March 29, 1774, C.O. 37 vol.36.
2. Bread and flour, overwhelmingly from the middle colonies and the Upper South, constituted, after tobacco, the major colonial commodity export, and their average annual value in the years 1768-72 was £412,000. D. Klingman, "The Significance of Grain in the Development of the Tobacco Colonies," *Journal of Economic History,* xxix, 2 (June 1969), pp. 268-278; J.F. Shepherd and G.M. Walton, *Shipping, Maritime Trade and Economic Development of Colonial North America,* (CUP, 1972).
3. Bruere, *op. cit.*
4. Wilfred B. Kerr, *Bermuda and the American Revolution: 1760-1783,* (Princeton University Press, 1936), describes it thus: "eighty to a hundred vessels were constantly at sea,

each manned by a skeleton crew of two whites and 4 negroes. Some of the boats were owned by their captains, a good many by better-off islanders who employed the crews.''

5. Kerr, *op. cit.,* p. 55.

6. Sabine, *Loyalists* vol. 2, p. 294: C.C. 37, v. 37, v. 38, v. 39; *Virginia Magazine of History and Biography,* vol. 15, p. 162; A.E. Merrill, ''Relations between Bermuda and American Colonies during the Revolutionary War,'' *Transactions of the Connecticut Academy of Arts and Sciences,* July 1907.

7. Tucker House Papers, Williamsburg, cited by W.B. Kerr, *op. cit.,* pp. 130-131; C.O. 37/39; Henry Tucker recommended ''passive obedience and non-resistance to Ministerial dictates,'' C.O. 37/39, fo. 129.

8. Henry C. Wilkinson, *Bermuda in the Old Empire,* (OUP, 1950), p. 435; Governor Hamilton recommended Bridger Goodrich to Lord Sidney, 18 October 1788, as a ''proper person'' to be a member of the Council of Bermuda, C.O. 37/40, fo. 210.

NOTES TO DAVIES

1. Oliver to Dartmouth, 28 November 1775 and 26 January 1776, Public Record Office, London, C.O.5/175, fos. 67, 73. Minutes of Council of Massachusetts, 25 to 30 October 1775, are filed with the first of these letters. All manuscript references in this paper are to the C.O.5 series.

2. Printed in K.G. Davies, ed., *Documents of the American Revolution,* Colonial Office Series, 1770–1783, Vol. XI (Dublin, 1976), pp. 203-205. Transcripts of most of the documents cited below are scheduled to appear in future volumes of this series.

3. *Ibid.,* p. 208.

4. Instructions in C.O.5/177, fo. 1.
5. Commissioners to Germain, 20 September 1776, C.O.5/177, fo. 35. It is not quite true that the appeal was without result. Governor Tryon collected the names of 3371 persons, including eleven blacks, who took an oath of allegiance in New York City early in 1777. Names in C.O.5/1108, fo. 69.
6. Historical Manuscripts Commission, *Stopford-Sackville Manuscripts,* Vol. II (London, 1910), p. 219.
7. Commissioners to Germain, 30 November 1776, and reply of 14 January 1777, C.O.5/177, fos. 45 and 55.
8. Tryon to Germain, 24 September 1776, C.O.5/1107, fo. 396.
9. Same to same, 1 December 1777, C.O.5/1108, fo. 167.
10. Martin to William Knox, 31 January 1778, C.O.5/155, fo. 208.
11. Instructions in C.O.5/180, fo. 3.
12. Commissioners to Germain, 7 July 1778, C.O.5/180, fo. 74.
13. Same to same, 21 September and 16 November 1778, C.O.5/180, fo. 145, and C.O.5/181, fo. 49.
14. Same to same (secret), 16 November 1778, C.O.5/181, fo. 90.
15. Instructions and blank commission to Campbell in C.O.5/181, fo. 94.
16. Germain to Clinton, 3 December 1778, C.O.5/96, fo. 189.
17. Same to same, 23 January 1779, C.O.5/97, fo. 12. Compare Germain to Campbell, 16 January 1779, C.O.5/182, fo. 5.
18. Germain to Wright, 31 March 1779, C.O.5/665, fo. 119.
19. Germain to Tryon, 1 April 1779, Germain to Robertson, 9 July 1779, C.O.5/1109, fos. 88, 140.
20. Germain to Clinton, 5 May 1779, C.O.5/97, fo. 214.
21. Same to same, 5 August 1779, C.O.5/98, fo. 65.
22. Germain to Wright, 31 March 1779, C.O.5/665, fo. 119.
23. Adam Ferguson to Knox, 26 March 1779, C.O.5/181, fo. 204, and enclosure at fo. 212.
24. Wright to Germain, 31 July 1779, C.O.5/665, fo. 141.
25. Same to same, 9 August 1779, C.O. 5/665, fo. 163.
26. Before he left England Wright had warned Germain that Georgia's first Assembly might not be loyal. Germain to Knox, 12 March 1779, in Historical Manuscripts Commission, *Various Collections,* Vol. VI (London, 1909), p. 156.

27. Wright to Germain, 20 January, 24 March, 6 April 1780, C.O.5/665, fos. 205, 230, 245.
28. Same to same, 20 December 1780, C.O.5/176, fo. 129.
29. Journal of Assembly, C.O.5/708; Acts, C.O.5/685.
30. Wright to Germain, 20 December 1780, C.O.5/176, fo. 129.
31. Wright to Clinton, 3 February 1780, C.O.5/665, fo. 219.
32. Germain to Wright, 3 January 1781, C.O.5/176, fo. 113.
33. Wright to Germain, 19 July 1780, C.O.5/665, fo. 302.
34. Same to same, 9 August 1779, C.O.5/665, fo. 163.
35. Same to same, 20 December 1780, C.O.5/176, fo. 129.
36. 'Golden dreams' is Sir Grey Cooper's phrase, in letter to Knox, 5 September 1780, printed in Historical Manuscripts Commission, *Various Collections,* Vol. VI, p. 172.
37. Simpson to Germain, 13 August 1780, C.O.5/178, fo. 56.
38. Simpson to Clinton, 15 May 1780, C.O.5/99, fo. 265.
39. Simpson to Germain, 25 September 1780, C.O.5/178, fo. 71.
40. Appointment of J.P.s, C.O.5/520, fo. 5, 5d; public health, C.O.5/519, fo. 4; poor, Simpson to Germain, 31 December 1780, C.O.5/178, fo. 75; circuit court clause, Simpson to Knox, 31 December 1780, C.O.5/178, fo. 84.
41. Germain to Bull, 4 April 1781, C.O.5/176, fo. 59.
42. Simpson to Germain, 30 August and 31 December 1780, C.O.5/178, fos. 68, 75.
43. Leigh to Germain, 25 February 1781, C.O.5/176, fo. 56.
44. Records of S.C. Board of Police, C.O.5/519-520.
45. Simpson to Knox, 31 December 1780, C.O.5/178, fo. 84.
46. Simpson to Germain, 30 August 1780, C.O.5/178, fo. 68.
47. Same to same, 31 December 1780, C.O.5/178, fo. 75.
48. Simpson to Knox, 31 December 1780, C.O.5/178, fo. 84; report on S.C. currency has survived as C.O.5/513.
49. Bull to Germain, 28 June 1781, C.O.5/176, fo. 71.
50. Simpson to Knox, 28 July 1781, C.O.5/178, fo. 172.
51. Same to same, 20 August 1781, C.O.5/178, fo. 189.
52. North Carolina: in correspondence between Governor Martin and Germain in 1780, C.O.5/176, fos. 20, 30. Virginia: petition of merchants trading to Virginia and Maryland, 3 August 1781, C.O.5/178, fo. 167. New Jersey: Governor Franklin to Germain, 20 December 1778, C.O.5/993, fo.

137. Rhode Island: Dudley to Germain, 13 March 1779, C.O.5/156, fo. 45.

53. Commissioners to Germain, 21 September 1778, C.O.5/180, fo. 145, enclosing proclamation. Same to same, 17 November 1778, C.O.5/181, fo. 35, with enclosures.

54. Germain to Robertson, 9 July 1779, C.O.5/1109, fo. 140.

55. Robertson to Germain, 1 July 1780, C.O.5/1110, fo. 134.

56. Same to same, 1 September 1780, C.O.5/1110, fo. 140.

57. Same to same, 28 January 1781, C.O.5/175, fo. 90.

58. Clinton to Germain, 9 March 1781, C.O.5/101, fo. 292.

59. Smith to Robertson, 9 May 1782, C.O.5/175, fo. 170.

60. Quoted in William B. Willcox, *Portrait of a General* (New York, 1964), p. 379.

61. Quoted in Kenneth Coleman, 'Restored Colonial Georgia, 1779–1782' in *Georgia Historical Quarterly,* Vol. 40, pp. 12-13.

62. Arbuthnot to Germain, 2 May 1780, in *Stopford-Sackville Manuscripts,* Vol. II, p. 161. This letter is said by Willcox to be misdated, *Portrait of a General,* p. 313, n. 2.

63. Clinton to Germain, 2 June 1780, C.O.5/99, fo. 286.

64. *Stopford-Sackville Manuscripts,* Vol. II, p. 168.

65. Simpson to Knox, 20 August 1781, enclosing Clinton to Simpson of 19 August 1781, C.O.5/178, fos. 189, 191.

66. Conversation between Clinton and Robertson, 23 January 1782, reported by latter, C.O.5/175, fo. 162; Robertson to Germain, 22 March 1782, C.O.5/175, fo. 145.

67. Commissioners to Germain, 25 January 1782, C.O.5/178, fo. 194.

68. Franklin to Germain, 6 November 1781, C.O.5/175, fo. 231.

69. Robertson to Shelburne, 9 May 1782, C.O.5/175, fo. 154.

70. Minutes of Council of New York, 1 March 1782, C.O.5/175, fo. 147.

NOTES TO UPTON

1. Report of August 10, 1784, in J. Eardley-Wilmot, *Historical View of the Commission for Enquiring into the Losses . . . of the American Loyalists* (London, 1815) 109-124; 56, 58-59.

2. *DNB,* I, 511-512; *Gentleman's Magazine,* 1819, Pt. II, Vol. 89, 569; *The Poetical Works of the Late Christopher Anstey Esq.,* (London, 1808).

3. L.F.S. Upton, ed., *The Diary and Selected Papers of Chief Justice William Smith,* 2 vols. (Toronto, 1963, 1965) II, 36, 45.

4. Woodruffe's Journal, American Philosophical Society, under dates April 18, 20, 24, 1786.

5. Anstey to Commissioners, May 3, 1786, February 22, 1787, AO 12/113 ff. 7-10, 60-66.

6. Report on New York, June 1786, AO 12/94 ff. 12-45.

7. Advertisement of May 9, 1786, AO 12/94 f. 1.

8. Anstey to Forster, June 30, 1787, AO 12/113, ff. 83-88.

9. Anstey to Commissioners, June 12, 1786, *ibid.,* ff. 13-17.

10. I have not found Anstey's instructions *per se,* and have reconstructed them from scattered references in the various reports.

11. Anstey to Commissioners, Saint John, April 22, 1786, AO 13/102 pt. 1, f. 571-572; Hunter to Anstey, May 17, 1786, AO 12/139.

12. Anstey to Commissioners, Halifax, September 12, 1786, AO 13/102 pt. 1, ff. 404-405.

13. List of papers sent June 10, 1787, *ibid.,* ff. 464-465.

14. Hunter to Anstey, May 17, 1786, *loc. cit.;* Return of List of Names, n.d. AO 12/113, ff. 29-30.

15. Anstey to Commissioners, May 3, 1786, *loc. cit.*

16. Anstey to Commissioners, August 2, 1786, AO 12/113, ff. 34-35.

17. Compiled from "Travelling Charges from Place to Place," AO 12/131.

18. Woodruffe's Journal, October 25, November 24, 1786.

19. *Ibid.,* December 27, 1786.

20. Anstey to Forster, February 22, March 20, 1787, AO 12/113, ff. 62-67.
21. Anstey to Forster, February 22, 1787, *loc. cit.*
22. Anstey to Commissioners, June 12, 1786, *loc. cit.*
23. Advertisement of May 9, 1786, *loc cit.*
24. Anstey to Commissioners, May 3, June 12, 1786, *loc. cit.*
25. Anstey to Forster, April 25, 1787, AO 12/113, ff. 68-73.
26. "Heads of Enquiry sent to Mr. Temple," n.d. [April, 1786], *ibid.,* ff. 2-3; Anstey to Forster, September 25, 1786, *ibid.,* ff. 44-51.
27. First Report on North Carolina, n.d., received June 12, 1787, AO 12/94, ff. 97-102; Report on South Carolina, May 30, 1788, AO 12/92, ff. 1-46.
28. Report on Massachusetts, November 4, 1787, AO 12/81, ff. 1-12.
29. Anstey to Forster, September 25, 1786, AO 12/113, ff. 44-51.
30. Report on Virginia, April 10, 1787, AO 12/94, ff. 86-95.
31. Report on Rhode Island, n.d., received March 5, 1788, AO 12/84, ff. 49-56.
32. Second Report on North Carolina, July 6, 1788, AO 12/91, ff. 4-9.
33. Report on Virginia, *loc. cit.*
34. Report on New York; Anstey to Commissioners, June 12, 1786, *loc. cit.*
35. First Report on North Carolina, *loc. cit.*
36. Anstey to Forster, June 30, 1787, AO 12/113, ff. 83-88.
37. Anstey to Forster, August 2, 1786, *ibid.,* ff. 36-39.
38. Anstey to Forster, June 13, September 25, 1786, *ibid.,* ff. 19-23, 44-51.
39. Bishop to Anstey, October 18, 1787, AO 12/84, f. 141; Anstey to Forster, June 30, 1787, *loc. cit.*
40. Anstey to Forster, September 25 1786, *loc. cit.*
41. Report on Pennsylvania, July 20, 1787, AO 12/95, ff. 1-20.
42. Report on New York, *loc. cit.*
43. Report on Massachusetts, *loc. cit.*
44. Report on New York, *loc. cit.*
45. Report on Pennsylvania, *loc. cit.*
46. Report on Maryland, April 20, 1787, AO 12/94, ff. 68-85.

47. Report on Pennsylvania; on Rhode Island, *loc. cit.*
48. AO 12/78 I & II, *passim.*
49. List, n.d., AO 12/86, ff. 1-41.
50. Anstey to Forster, June 6, 1786, AO 12/113, ff. 32-33; lists at AO 12/86, ff. 44-80, AO 12/87, ff. 30-35.
51. Report on New York, *loc. cit.*
52. Report on South Carolina, *loc. cit.*
53. Report on Pennsylvania, *loc. cit.*
54. Report on South Carolina, *loc. cit.*
55. Report on Massachusetts, *loc. cit.*
56. Report on Pennsylvania; on New York, *loc. cit.*
57. Report on Pennsylvania, *loc. cit.*
58. Report on Virginia, *loc. cit.*
59. Woodruffe's Journal, December 11, 1787.
60. Anstey to Commissioners, June 6, 1786, *loc. cit.*
61. Report on Massachusetts, *loc. cit.*
62. Report on Virginia, *loc. cit.*
63. First and Second Reports on North Carolina, *loc. cit.*
64. Report on Rhode Island, *loc. cit.*
65. Report on South Carolina, *loc. cit.*
66. Wilmot, *Historical View,* 182, 67, 192.

NOTES TO CHRISTIE

1. L.B. Namier, *The Structure of Politics at the Accession of George III* (2 v., London, 1929), I, v-vi; Julia Namier, *Lewis Namier. A Biography* (Oxford, 1971), p. 112.
2. Thomas Whately, *The Regulations lately made concerning the colonies and the taxes imposed on them considered* (London, 1765), pp. 5-23 gave an authoritative exposition of this policy.
3. The development of these concepts has been traced in Klaus E. Knorr, *British Colonial Theories, 1570–1850* (London, 1944; repr. 1963).

4. *A Discourse about Trade* (London, 1690), p. 166, cited Knorr, pp. 80-1.
5. *Discourses on the Publick Revenues and on the Trade of England* (London, 1698), II, 204, cited Knorr, p. 106.
6. *The Regulations lately made concerning the colonies and the taxes imposed on them considered* (London, 1765), p. 89.
7. *Op. cit.*, pp. 58-9.
8. *Op. cit.*, p. 88.
9. *The Regulations lately made concerning the colonies . . .*, pp. 47-50, 54-6, 69.
10. For these comparisons see Judith Blow Williams, *British Commercial Policy and Trade Expansion* (Oxford, 1972), pp. 186-7, 150, 177, 78, 196, citing figures from Sir Charles Whitworth, *State of the Trade of Great Britain . . .* (London, 1776). I am grateful to Dr. Julian Gwyn for drawing attention to the fact that the re-export trade in tobacco from Scotland to France is not included in these figures.
11. 'The Parliamentary Diaries of Nathaniel Ryder,' ed. by P.D.G. Thomas, *Camden Miscellany, XXIII* (Royal Historical Society, London, 1919), p. 234.
12. *The Regulations lately made concerning the colonies . . .*, pp. 89, 92.
13. *The Regulations lately made concerning the colonies . . .*, pp. 74-5, 84-5.
14. R.W. Van Alstyne, *Empire and Independence, The International History of the American Revolution* (New York, 1965), p. 1; Richard Koebner, *Empire* (Cambridge, 1961), pp. 88-9.
15. *The Regulations lately made concerning the colonies . . .*, pp. 39-40.
16. Sir William Blackstone, *Commentaries on the Laws of England* (4 v., Oxford, 1773), I, 106-9.
17. *The Regulations lately made concerning the colonies . . .*, p. 40.
18. James Otis, *The Rights of the British Colonies Asserted and Proved* (Boston, 1764), p. 12, cited in Bernard Bailyn, *Pamphlets of the American Revolution, 1750–1775,* volume I (Cambridge, Mass., 1965), p. 426.

19. *The Fitch Papers,* volume II, Connecticut Historical Society, *Collections,* XVIII (Hartford, Conn., 1920), pp. 337-40.
20. Edmund S. and Helen M. Morgan, *The Stamp Act Crisis: Prologue to Revolution* (2nd edn., New York, 1963), p. 326.
21. *The Fitch Papers,* volume II, Connecticut Historical Society, *Collections,* XVIII, p. 339.
22. *Autobiography and political correspondence of Augustus Henry, third duke of Grafton,* ed. Sir William R. Anson (London, 1898), p. 127; Thomas Townshend in debate, 8 Feb. 1769, *Sir Henry Cavendish's Debates,* ed. John Wright (2 v., London, 1841-3), I, 213.
23. Ian R. Christie and Benjamin W. Labaree, *Empire or Independence. A British-American dialogue on the coming of the American Revolution* (New York, 1976), chapters VII and VIII.
24. *The Correspondence of General Thomas Gage . . .,* ed. by C.E. Carter (new impr., 2 v., Yale, 1969), I, 291-2, II, 589-90.
25. *The Parliamentary History of England,* VIII, 1200-1.
26. For these parallels see Ian R. Christie, 'The Historians' Quest for the American Revolution,' in *Statesmen, Scholars and Merchants, Essays in eighteenth-century history presented to Dame Lucy Sutherland,* edited by Anne Whiteman, J.S. Bromley, and P.G.M. Dickson (Oxford, 1973), pp. 197-9.

NOTES TO FELLOWS

1. *Population in History*. (London: Edward Arnold, 1965) p. 8.
2. Introductory working papers, #1-4, are available. Contact the author at the University of New Brunswick, Fredericton, N.B., Canada.
3. Historical record linkage is now a special area of study within the over-all area of quantitative history. See Ian Winchester, "A Brief Survey of the algorithmic, mathematical, and philosophical literature relevant to historical record linkage," Chap. 6, in *Identifying People in the Past*, E.A. Wrigley, ed., (London: Edward Arnold, 1973), pp. 128-156, as a useful starting point.
4. The intention of this study parallels, at least initially, that of the research project, *Reconstitution de la population Canadienne—française à l'époque préindustrielle,* Hubert Charboneau and Jacques Légaré, Université de Montreal. A list of additional research projects in quantitative history under way in Canada is given in *Histoire Sociale/Social History,* 7 (1974), pp. 165-169.
5. The Loyalist settlers in Upper Canada petitioned initially for freehold tenure, and only later began agitation for political rights.
6. Copy, Provincial Archives of New Brunswick, MYY 429.
7. (Moncton, N.B.: The Author), pp. 255-345.
8. (Halifax: Public Archives, 1937).
9. *The Centennial of the Settlement of Upper Canada by the United Empire Loyalists, 1784-1884.* (Toronto: Rose Publishing Company, 1885). Appendix B., pp. 129-332.
10. (Lambertville, N.J.: Hunterdon House, 1973).
11. Annual reports are available on the Programme for Loyalist Studies, Canadian Committee, University of New Brunswick, Fredericton, N.B., Canada.

THE LOYALISTS:
A BRIEF BIBLIOGRAPHY

The first printed volumes on the Loyalists appeared as early as 1780 in Joseph Galloway's *Historical and Political Reflections on the Rise and Progress of The American Rebellion,* and in 1788 in his *The Claim of the American Loyalists,* both of them written as part of the vicious post-mortem on Britain's failure in the War, then blamed primarily and firmly on the brothers Howe. There are understanding references to the plight of the "offerers" in a number of contemporary histories of the War of Independence, notably in George Chalmers, *Political Annals of the Present United Colonies* (London 1780), Charles Stedman, *The History of the Origin, Progress and Termination of the American War* (2 Vols, (London 1794), and David Ramsay, *History of the American Revolution* (2 Vols, London 1793). Jonathan Boucher's *Reminiscences of an American Loyalist 1738-1789* was not published until 1925; Samuel Curwen's *Journal and Letters 1775-1784* was first published (ed. by his great-grandson George A. Ward) in 1842, but in a much superior edition in 1972 (ed. Andrew Oliver, Harvard U.P.).

In 1815 John Eardly-Wilmot published his account of the work of the Claims Commissioners, *Historical View of the Commission for Enquiring into the Losses, Services and Claims of the American Loyalists;* with this compare H.E. Egerton (ed.) *The Royal Commission on the Losses and Services of the American Loyalists 1783-1785* (OUP 1915). Wallace Brown has worked through the

Audit Office papers of the Claimants (AO 12 and 13) and analysed them thoroughly, in his *The King's Friends* (Providence 1966) and *The Good Americans* (N.Y. 1965); compare also Mary Beth Norton, *The British Americas* (Little Brown 1970). For a critical assessment of these studies see an article by Eugene Fingerhut, "Uses and Abuses of the American Loyalist Claims: a Critique of Quantitative Analyses," *William and Mary Quarterly, 3rd Series,* XXV, (April 1968), pp. 245-58.

It is not of course, true to say that there has been a total neglect of the Loyalists. The first American historian to give the Loyalists their due was that gifted amateur Lorenzo Sabine who published in 1847 his biographical sketches which he amplified seventeen years later. It is a work to which there is still no rival, the first piece of oral history ever attempted and done with dedication. It could well be argued that one of the real needs in the field is a new Sabine, a new biographical dictionary of the Loyalists along Namier-like lines. Moses C. Tyler published in 1897 his *Literary History of the American Revolution* and also a famous article in the first number of the *A.H.R.* in 1895 on the Loyalists. This reflected the interest of his period in Anglo-American relations, and had indeed something of a WASP character. In his eyes "The Tories of the Revolution" had among them "a very considerable portion of the most refined, thoughtful and conscientious people in the colonies." But it was an attempt to portray what he called the inward history of the revolution, the history of its ideas, motives and passions; he had the great merit of shifting the emphasis from the purely political story to intellectual relations, and he brought remarkable qualities of objectivity and grace to that task. But it is still true to say that there is only one coherent study of the political role of the Loyalists other than William Nelson's essay, and that is Claude Van Tyne's *The Loyalists in the American Revolution* (N.Y. 1902). His scholarship is open to some criticism, and he has no bibliography; and he appears to have made very little use of the transcripts of Loyalist claims which Benjamin Stevens had already listed from his work in the P.R.O. in the 1880s. But his book was the first clear study of the Loyalists, and it is perhaps a tribute to his objectivity that his school text book had the merit of being banned in the schools of Battle Creek, Michigan, because in his

writing and for the first time there was a departure from the
straight re- telling of the Patriot story.

In the half century that followed Van Tyne's book there were a
few studies of the Loyalists, state by state: notable among then
were James Stark's study of the Loyalists in Massachusetts,
published in 1910; Otis Hammond's *The New Hampshire Loyalists*
in 1917; Edward Jones's study of the Loyalists in New Jersey in
1927; and Isaac Harrell's study of the Virginia Loyalists published
in 1926. But perhaps in this period the most significant contributions were the biography of Jared Ingersoll by Lawrence Gipson in
1920, and the series of articles by Wilbur Siebert of Ohio State
University. In the same period a number of sources became
available. In 1905 the Archives of Ontario published the notes of
some of the commissioners on the claims of the Loyalists. A decade
later the notes of D.P. Coke, another of the commissioners, were
edited and published in London. Then in the 1920s and 1930s Edward Jones published his study of Massachusetts Loyalists, and a
number of Loyalist diaries and journals appeared; De Mond's *The
Loyalists in North Carolina* was published in 1940.

In the last few years there has been an even more dramatic
change. In 1961 there appeared a scholarly edition of Peter Oliver's
Origin and Progress, and William Nelson's essay *The American
Tory* (OUP), which gives however, little guidance on sources, and
draws almost exclusively on printed diaries. Since then we have had
L.S.F. Upton's admirable edition of Chief Justice William Smith's
Diary (1963/65) and his biography of Smith (*The Loyal Whig,*
1969) and Robert Calhoon's massive and extremely useful *The
Loyalists in Revolutionary America 1760–1781* (Harcourt Brace
Jovanovich, N.Y. 1973)

To these titles it should be added that there have been from Paul
Smith in his *Loyalists and Redcoats* (1964) and from Piers Mackesy
in *The War in America* (1964) for the first time two assessments of
the impact of the Loyalists on the actual campaigns. To this subject, John Shy of the University of Michigan, Ann Arbor, has
recently made a major contribution. (*A People Numerous and
Armed,* OUP 1976). It would be a serious error of omission not to
cite here the notable history written by Bernard Bailyn of Harvard.
In 1964 he produced the first volume of his pamphlets on the

American Revolution, with its notable introductory essay "The Transforming Radicalism of the American Revolution" (Harvard University Press) and in 1975, he produced what might well be regarded as one of the best pieces of recent Loyalist scholarship in his study *The Ordéal of Thomas Hutchinson,* (Harvard University Press), a brilliant interpretation of the state of mind of the last Loyalist Governor of the colony of Massachusetts. It draws heavily on the diary and papers of Governor Hutchinson, both in Boston and in the British Museum, and, alongside Leonard Labaree's study of the Loyalists in the *Proceedings of American Antiquarian Society* (LIV 1944) becomes essential reading for an understanding of the intellectual assumptions that the Loyalists were making. It should be compared with Dr. Ann Condon's paper "Marching to a Different Drummer" in this Symposium.

NOTES ON CONTRIBUTORS

Ann Condon
Dr Condon received her Ph.D. from Harvard University in 1975. She was an Honorary Fellow at the Institute for United States Studies, University of London in 1975-76, and is a research associate at the University of New Brunswick.

Francis Jennings
Francis Jennings is Director of the Center for the History of the American Indian at the Newberry Library, Chicago, Illinois, and author of *The Invasion of America: Indians, Colonialism, and the Cant of Conquest,* published for the Institute of Early American History and Culture by the University of North Carolina Press, Chapel Hill, N.Ca., 1975.

Peter Marshall
Peter Marshal is a graduate of Oxford and Yale. He has taught at the Universities of Bristol, California, Berkeley, and McGill, before assuming his present post of Professor of American History and Institutions at the University of Manchester. He is the author of some dozen articles in the period of the Revolution.

George Rawlyk
George Rawlyk is Professor of History at Queen's University, Kingston, Canada. He is the author of *Yankees at Louisbourg* (1967) and *Nova Scotia's Massachusetts* (1973) and coauthor with Gordon Stewart of *A People Highly Favoured of God.* He is now working on the Loyalist impact on Eastern Upper Canada.

Wallace Brown
Wallace Brown is Professor of History at the University of New Brunswick, Fredericton, New Brunswick, Canada, and has published widely on the American Loyalists including *The Good Americans: The Loyalists of the American Revolution* (William Morrow, New York, 1969). He is now working on a sequel that will deal with the Loyalists in exile. Since 1975, he has been chairman of the Canadian Committee for Loyalist Studies and Publications.

Esmond Wright
Esmond Wright is Director of the Institute of United States Studies and Professor of American History in the University of London; British Editor of Loyalist Papers Project; author of *Fabric of Freedom* (Hill and Wang, 1961) and other books; editor of *Causes and Consequences of the American Revolution* (Quadrangle Books, Chicago, 1966) and *A Tug of Loyalties* (Athlone Press, 1974)

K.G. Davies
Kenneth Gordon Davies has held appointments at the Public Record Office, L.S.E., and Oxford. His publications include *The Royal African Company* (1957) and *North Atlantic World in the 17th Century* (1974). Since 1970 he has edited *Documents of the American Revolution* (Colonial Office Series), of which ten volumes have been published.

Leslie Upton
Leslie Upton is a Professor of History at the University of British Columbia. He read Modern History at Oxford and took his doctorate at the University of Minnesota. He has been a student of the Loyalists for some twenty years.

Ian Christie
Ian Christie is Professor of Modern History at University College, London and is currently Chairman of Department. He is the joint author in collaboration with Benjamin Woods Labaree, of *Empire or Independence. A British–American dialogue on the coming of the American Revolution* (1976). He has published a number of books and articles on late 18th century British policies including *The End of North's Ministry 1780–1782* (1958) and *Wilkes, Wyvill and Reform* (1962).

Jo-Ann Carr Fellows
Jo-Ann Carr Fellows is a graduate of the University of New Brunswick, Fredericton, Canada, and the University of Waterloo, Ontario. She is presently a research associate with the Loyalist Studies Programme, University of New Brunswick. Her specialty is the application of quantative methods in history.

INDEX